Symbiosis: Utilizing Symbiotic Leadership™ to Guide and Improve Relationships.

By Brian Patrick Haywood

© 2024 Brian Haywood. All rights reserved.

U.S. Copyright Registration Number: TXu 2-485-824

No part of this publication may be reproduced, stored in a retrieval system, or transmitted in any form or by any means—electronic, mechanical, photocopying, recording, or otherwise—without prior written permission of the publisher, except in the case of brief quotations embodied in critical articles or reviews.

ISBN (Paperback): 978-1-968440-00-8 / 978-1-968440-03-9
ISBN (Digital / eBook): 978-1-968440-01-5
ISBN (Hardback): 978-1-968440-02-2

Published by Scale Matrix LLC
An imprint of Knight Publishing
www.MySymbiosis.com

Cover and interior design by Scale Matrix, LLC

Symbiotic Relationship Theory™, Symbiotic Leadership Framework™, and Symbiotic Workplace Model™ are trademarks of Brian Haywood. All rights reserved.

This is a work of original nonfiction. All frameworks, methodologies, and concepts are the intellectual property of the author and publisher unless otherwise cited.

Printed in the United States of America
First Edition

Symbiosis: Utilizing Symbiotic Leadership™ to Guide and Improve Relationships

Table of Contents

Dedication 12
Purpose of This Book 13
Preface 14
Definition of Terms 16
Introduction 17
    Why Symbiosis Matters Now 17
    The Importance of Symbiosis in Modern Relationships ... 20
    Integrating Leadership Principles and Relationship Dynamics 20
Chapter 1: What is Symbiosis? 22
    1.1 The Timeless Power of Symbiosis 22
        1.1.1 Symbiosis in Successful Business Partnerships . 25
        1.1.2 Symbiosis in Historical Marriages and Relationships 29
        1.1.3 Symbiosis in International Alliances 30
        Conclusion: The Timeless Power of Symbiosis 34
    1.2 The Counter to Symbiosis 35
        1.2.1 Parasitism: The One-Sided Relationship 36
        1.2.2 Exploitation: Manipulating for Personal Gain 40
        1.2.3 Unchecked Competition: Destroying Relationships Through Rivalry 43
        1.2.4 The Consequences of Counter-Symbiotic Relationships 46
        Conclusion: Guarding Against Counter-Symbiosis 47
    1.3 The Benefits of a Symbiotic Relationship 48

- 1.3.1 Mutual Growth and Development 48
- 1.3.2 Increased Trust and Emotional Security 51
- 1.3.3 Sustainable Stability and Resilience 53
- 1.3.4 Enhanced Creativity and Innovation 55
- 1.3.5 Legacy and Long-Term Impact 56
- Conclusion: The Transformative Power of Symbiosis .. 58
- 1.4 Symbiosis in Nature 60
  - 1.4.1 Mutualism: A Blueprint for Win-Win Relationships 61
  - 1.4.2 Commensalism: One Benefits Without Harming the Other 66
  - 1.4.3 Parasitism: One Benefits at the Other's Expense 70
  - 1.4.4 Consequences of Parasitism: The Price of Imbalance 77
  - Conclusion: Recognizing and Eliminating Parasitic Relationships 78
- 1.5 Symbiosis in the Universe 79
  - 1.5.1 The Sun and Earth: Life-Sustaining Interdependence 80
  - 1.5.2 The Moon and Earth: Gravitational Harmony and Stability 83
  - 1.5.3 Stellar Life Cycle: Birth, Death, and Regeneration 85
  - 1.5.4 Planetary Orbits and Gravitational Balance: Order in Chaos 88
  - 1.5.5 Black Holes and Event Horizons: The Consequences of Imbalance 91

Conclusion: Cosmic Lessons for Thriving Relationships 94

1.6 The Role of Reciprocity: Cultivating Mutual Benefit in Relationships 95

    1.6.1 Understanding Reciprocity: The Foundation of Mutual Exchange 96

    1.6.2 Reciprocity in Business: Building Trust and Loyalty 98

    1.6.3 Reciprocity in Personal Relationships: Strengthening Emotional Bonds 100

    1.6.4 Reciprocity in Leadership: Empowering Teams and Organizations 101

    1.6.5 The Consequences of a Lack of Reciprocity 104

    1.6.6 Cultivating a Culture of Reciprocity: Practical Steps 106

    Conclusion: Reciprocity as the Lifeblood of Thriving Relationships 109

1.7 Mutual Growth and Accountability: Sustaining Symbiotic Relationships 110

    1.7.1 Understanding Mutual Growth: A Commitment to Shared Development 111

    1.7.2 Accountability: Safeguarding Integrity and Excellence 114

    1.7.3 The Intersection of Mutual Growth and Accountability 117

    1.7.4 Consequences of Neglecting Mutual Growth and Accountability 119

    1.7.5 Practical Strategies for Cultivating Mutual Growth and Accountability 121

Conclusion: The Power of Mutual Growth and Accountability 124

Chapter 1 Recap: The Importance of Symbiosis in Modern Relationships 125

Chapter 2: The Different Types of Relationships 133

2.1 Family: The First Environment for Symbiosis 134

    2.1.1 Mutual Contribution in Family Relationships 134

    2.1.2 Reciprocity and Respect Across Generations ... 137

    2.1.3 Accountability and Grace in Family Structures . 139

    2.1.4 When Symbiosis Breaks Down: Family Disintegration 141

    Chapter 2.1 Summary: Family – The First Environment for Symbiosis 142

2.2 Friendship: A Chosen Symbiotic Relationship 145

    2.2.1 The Power of Mutual Investment 146

    2.2.2 Reciprocity in Emotional Support 147

    2.2.3 Accountability Among Peers 149

    2.2.4 Loyalty and Consistency Over Time 150

    2.2.5 When Friendship Becomes Parasitic 152

    Chapter 2.2 Summary: Friendship - A Chosen Symbiotic Relationship 154

2.3 Love/Partnerships: Building Covenant through Symbiosis 156

    2.3.1 Emotional Reciprocity and Safety 158

    2.3.2 Shared Purpose and Vision 159

    2.3.3 Conflict Resolution and Accountability 161

    2.3.4 Physical Intimacy as Mutual Giving 161

2.3.5 Loyalty, Commitment, and Covenant............... 163

2.3.6 Recognizing and Healing Unhealthy Attachments
.... 164

Chapter 2.3 Summary: Love/Partnerships: Building
Covenant through Symbiosis 166

2.4 Co-workers: Collaborating Through Symbiotic
Leadership™ 168

2.4.1 Mutual Contribution in Team Environments 168

2.4.2 Communication and Psychological Safety 171

2.4.3 Accountability and Integrity in Professional
Relationships... 172

2.4.4 Navigating Competition and Collaboration 174

2.4.5 Conflict and Restoration in the Workplace 176

2.4.6 Recognizing and Addressing Toxic Coworker
Relationships... 178

Chapter 2.4 Summary: Coworkers Collaborating
Through Symbiotic Leadership™.............................. 180

2.5 Mentorship/Coaching: Symbiosis Through Guidance
.... 182

2.5.1 The Symbiotic Flow of Knowledge and Growth . 183

2.5.2 Trust and Accountability in Mentorship 184

2.5.3 Coaching for Alignment and Confidence.......... 185

Chapter 2.5 Summary: Mentorship/Coaching -
Symbiosis Through Guidance 186

2.6 Daily Interactions: Practicing Micro-Symbiosis....... 187

2.6.1 Choosing Respect in Every Encounter 188

2.6.2 Daily Kindness as Cultural Currency................ 189

2.6.3 Micro-Symbiosis in a Digital World 189

Chapter 2.6 Summary: Daily Interactions - Practicing Micro-Symbiosis 191

Chapter 2 Summary: The Different Types of Relationships 192

Chapter 3: Reimagining Leadership Through Symbiosis ... 197

3.1 Introducing Symbiotic Relationship Theory™ (SRT) and Symbiotic Workplace Model™ (SWM) 200

   3.1.1 What is Symbiotic Relationship Theory™ (SRT)? 200

   3.1.2 What is the Symbiotic Workplace Model™ (SWM)? 202

   3.1.3 The Difference Between SRT and Classical Theories 203

   3.1.4 Why a Symbiotic Relationship Theory™ & Symbiotic Workplace Model™ Is Needed 203

3.2 Comparison: SRT vs. Maslow's Hierarchy of Needs. 204

   3.2.1 Where Maslow Ends, SRT Begins 205

   3.2.2 SRT's Relational Expansion of Maslow's Categories 206

   3.2.3 Leadership Application: Maslow vs. SRT in the Workplace 207

Chapter 3.2 Summary: SRT vs. Maslow's Hierarchy of Needs 207

3.3 SRT/SWM vs. McGregor's Theory X and Theory Y 208

   3.3.1 From Assumption to Interaction 210

   3.3.2 Key Comparison Points 212

   3.3.3 SRT/SWM's Contribution: Beyond Binary 213

   3.3.4 Theory X and Y Comparison to SRT/SWM 214

Chapter 3.3 Summary: SRT/SWM vs. McGregor's Theory X and Theory Y 215

3.4 SRT vs. McClelland's Needs Theory 216

    3.4.1 Side-by-Side Comparison: Needs Theory & Symbiotic Relationship Theory™ 219

    3.4.2 Interdependence Reframes the Three Needs ... 219

    3.4.3 SRT in the Workplace vs. Individual Motivation Models 221

    Chapter 3.4 Summary: SRT vs. McClelland's Needs Theory 222

3.5 SRT/SWM and Emotional Intelligence (Goleman) 222

    3.5.1 EQ vs. SRT: From Inward Reflection to Relational Culture 224

    3.5.2 How SRT/SWM Operationalize Emotional Intelligence 225

    Chapter 3.5 Summary: SRT/SWM and Emotional Intelligence (Goleman) 228

3.6 SRT vs. Servant Leadership 229

    3.6.1 Core Comparison: Servant Leadership vs. Symbiotic Relationship Theory™ 230

    3.6.2 From Leader-Centric to Ecosystemic 231

    3.6.3 Practical Application 232

    Chapter 3.6 Summary: SRT vs. Servant Leadership... 233

3.7: Chapter Summary – Reframing the Leadership Conversation? 234

    3.7.1 What We've Learned 235

    3.7.2 Comparative Overview: Classic Theories vs. SRT/SWM 236

Chapter 3 Closing Thought 237
Chapter 4: Symbiotic Leadership™ Scaling Relationship-Driven Growth 240
   4.1 The Three Spheres of the Symbiotic Model 241
   4.2 What is Symbiotic Leadership™? 242
      4.2.1 Key Characteristics of Symbiotic Leadership™ . 244
      4.2.2 Why Symbiotic Leadership™ Is Needed Now 244
      4.2.3 The Relationship to SRT and SWM 245
   4.3 The 12 Principles of Symbiotic Leadership™ 246
   4.4: Application Across Scales 254
      4.4.1 Symbiotic Leadership Principles Matrix™ 255
   4.5: The Three Layers of the Symbiotic Model............... 257
      4.5.1. Symbiotic Relationship Theory™ (SRT) 258
      4.5.2. Symbiotic Workplace Model™ (SWM).............. 258
      4.5.3. Symbiotic Leadership Framework™ (SLF) 259
      4.5.4 The Fractal Alignment™ 261
Chapter 5: What We've Built 263
   5.1 We Introduced the Three Spheres of Symbiotic Leadership™: 264
   5.2 Real-World Implications of Adopting This Model..... 266
      5.2 Summary 269
   5.3 A Call for Courage and Cultural Renewal................ 270
      5.3 Summary 273
   5.4 Reflection Questions for Leaders and Organizations 273
      5.4.1 Self-Reflection Questions for Individual Leaders 274

5.4.2 Team/Organizational Culture Questions 275

5.5 Tools – Equipping Your Culture for Symbiotic Leadership™ 276

Chapter 6: Leading the Future with Symbiotic Leadership™ 279

6.1 A Commission of Conviction, Culture, and Calling . 279

6.2 The Invitation to Transformation 279

6.3 Visualization of Symbiotic Leadership Framework™ 281

Glossary 301

Dedication

This book is dedicated to:
Hilda Lagunes — a housekeeper who became my best friend.
Richard Ross — a best friend who became my brother.
Tanja Zapp — a stranger who became my family.

A special mention goes to:
Dr. Angela Patrick, my professor, who became a mentor and a pillar of moral support.

Eric and Chrystal Haberman, extraordinary friends and mentors whose wisdom and care I value wholeheartedly.

Sharita Herrera, my first college professor, who sparked this journey and who I can honestly say is the best of the best of the best — of the best!

From the bottom of my heart, thank you.

To Brian Haywood

The child, the teenager, the young adult. The barber, the graphic designer, the car salesman, the project manager, the college professor, and now, the doctor. For all you've learned, loved, lost, and let go of to arrive at this moment, where you can now share a new perspective that just might help someone else. To the man you are today: Thank you!

Purpose of This Book

Symbiosis: Utilizing Symbiotic Leadership™ to Guide and Improve Relationships introduces a comprehensive 3-dimensional framework grounded in Fractal Alignment™, integrating Symbiotic Leadership™, Symbiotic Relationship Theory™ (SRT), and the Symbiotic Workplace Model™ (SWM). This book explores the historical foundations of symbiosis, dissects various relationship dynamics, and examines leadership and psychological theories that inform meaningful, effective human connection.

Through both conceptual exploration and real-world application, this work presents symbiosis not merely as a biological principle but also as a transformative leadership model. It provides tools, insights, and case studies that demonstrate the power of mutual growth, shared purpose, and relational accountability in strengthening teams, organizations, and communities.

As you move through these pages, you'll find practical principles and leadership tools designed to deepen trust, clarify communication, and empower collaborative progress. Whether you're leading a team, influencing culture, or seeking better-aligned relationships in the workplace, this book affirms that leadership is not about titles; it's about intentional influence. We all have a role to play in cultivating healthy, meaningful relationships at every level of life and leadership.

Preface

This book didn't begin as a theory. It began as survival.

Long before the charts, models, and leadership language, there was only life, raw, unfiltered, and often uncertain. I stood behind a barber's chair, honed the art of persuasion in a car dealership, built brands as a graphic designer, led global teams as a project manager, and mentored students as a college professor. In every season, the relationships I encountered shaped me. Some nurtured growth. Some exposed pain. All taught me something.

Over time, I noticed a pattern—an unseen thread running through the healthiest, most life-giving relationships I had ever experienced, both personal and professional. They weren't perfect, but they shared something in common: mutual respect, collective growth, accountability, and a sense of alignment. It was symbiotic.

This realization didn't just change how I led, it changed how I lived.
What if we could develop a leadership theory and organizational model centered on that idea?
What if the workplace, like nature, could flourish through systems of reciprocity rather than hierarchy alone? What if leadership could become less about control and more about connection?

That's how Symbiotic Relationship Theory™, the Symbiotic Workplace Model™, and the Symbiotic Leadership Framework™ were developed. Together, they form the backbone of this book—a 3-dimensional, scalable approach I've named Fractal Alignment™. From the C-suite to the frontline, this framework helps align people, purpose, and performance through relationships grounded in mutual trust and shared accountability.

This book is for both leaders and non-leaders. You don't need a title to influence culture or change the atmosphere of a room. You simply need to lead intentionally, empathetically, and in alignment with something greater than ego. Whether you're managing a team, building a business, raising a family, or trying to rebuild what was broken, this book is for you.

Each chapter invites you to see leadership not as a position, but as a posture. To apply principles that scale across industries and relationships. And to rediscover the transformational power of connection in a disconnected world.

If even one principle in these pages shifts your thinking, your workplace, or your relationships for the better, then this work has done its job.

Let's lead differently. Let's lead together. Let's lead symbiotically.

— Brian Haywood

Definition of Terms

Term	Definition
Symbiotic Relationship Theory™ (SRT)	A leadership-based relational theory that emphasizes mutual growth, shared purpose, and reciprocal accountability across all types of relationships.
Symbiotic Workplace Model™ (SWM)	A scalable model for aligning organizational structure and behavior through relational leadership practices that promote collaboration, equity, and shared outcomes.
Symbiotic Leadership™	A leadership approach rooted in empathy, alignment, accountability, and the development of others through trust and mutual benefit.
Symbiotic Leadership Principles™	Twelve core principles designed to guide relational leadership at all levels, from C-suite to individual contributors.
Fractal Alignment™	A visual and philosophical concept showing how relational principles scale across different levels—from cosmic systems to workplace teams—based on repeating, aligned patterns.
Relational Symmetry™	The balanced structure within relationships that ensures mutual respect, psychological safety, and equitable contribution from all parties involved.
SRT → SWM → SLF	The foundational sequence of the Symbiosis system: theory (SRT), applied model (SWM), and the resulting leadership framework (SLF).

Introduction

In a world where relationships form the cornerstone of personal and professional success, symbiosis offers a powerful lens through which we can analyze and enhance human interactions. Derived from the Greek words syn (meaning "together") and biosis (meaning "life"), symbiosis refers to the mutually beneficial relationship between two entities, fostering growth and survival. While traditionally associated with biology, the principles of symbiosis extend far beyond the natural world, providing profound insights into how individuals, families, teams, and communities can thrive when they engage in reciprocal relationships built on trust, accountability, and mutual benefit.

When applied intentionally, leadership theories are often studied in the context of guiding organizations and inspiring teams, and can have a profound impact on personal and professional relationships. Leaders who embody principles such as emotional intelligence, servant leadership, and transformational leadership cultivate environments where relationships blossom. Similarly, relationship theories such as attachment theory, love languages, and social exchange theory offer frameworks for understanding the nuances of interpersonal dynamics. By bridging these disciplines, a symbiotic relationship emerges as a guiding principle that enhances connection, trust, and mutual growth across all facets of life.

Why Symbiosis Matters Now

In today's fast-paced world, the imperative for relational resilience has become more pressing than ever. While technology offers instantaneous connections, it frequently results in a profound sense of isolation among individuals. In professional environments, organizations often focus solely on quantifiable outputs, inadvertently overlooking the vital importance of emotional safety and psychological well-being. Leaders face the daunting challenge of driving high performance, yet many find themselves equipped with insufficient resources to foster an atmosphere of belonging, nurture trust, and promote shared accountability among team members.

This growing fragmentation has a cost:

- Burnout is rising across industries.
- Loneliness and disconnection are now classified as public health concerns.
- Organizational trust gaps threaten long-term innovation and loyalty.

Symbiosis is the antidote.

It stands as a timeless yet remarkably modern reminder that we are inherently meant to succeed not in isolation, but within a community. Our genuine potential flourishes when we support one another, boldly investing in each other's successes, lending a hand during shared struggles, and aligning our deepest aspirations with our everyday actions. United, we create a tapestry of shared strength and purpose, showcasing the beauty of mutual support in our endeavors.

Symbiosis teaches us that:

- Healthy ecosystems mirror healthy organizations: interdependent, diverse, and resilient.
- Leadership is not about power over others, but partnership with others.

- Sustainable growth, whether personal or professional, is relational at its root.

This book is a blueprint for that renewal.
By exploring how Symbiotic Relationship Theory™ (SRT), the Symbiotic Workplace Model™ (SWM), and the Symbiotic Leadership Framework™ (SLF) operate across every level of life, we are reclaiming the lost art of intentional, reciprocal leadership and living.

You are not simply invited to read about these principles; you are welcome to build with them, lead through them, and transform the spaces you inhabit.

The future belongs to those who can cultivate symbiosis.

This book prepares you to be one of them.

The Importance of Symbiosis in Modern Relationships

Modern relationships face unprecedented challenges within families, friendships, partnerships, and the workplace. Digital communication has fostered global connections but, paradoxically, has also led to increased isolation and superficial engagement. Leaders in both personal and professional settings are often tasked with navigating these complexities, making it imperative to adopt a mindset that prioritizes mutual benefit and shared accountability. When individuals engage with others through the lens of symbiosis, they create opportunities for deeper trust, more meaningful connections, and sustainable growth.

Integrating Leadership Principles and Relationship Dynamics

Exploring the connection between leadership principles and relationship theories reveals key insights into cultivating thriving symbiotic relationships. Models like Maslow's Hierarchy of Needs, McGregor's Theory X and Theory Y, and McClelland's Needs Theory stress the significance of acknowledging individual needs, motivations, and aspirations. When these principles are applied across different relationships, whether between partners, colleagues, mentors, or mentees, they foster environments where everyone feels valued, listened to, and empowered. Furthermore, incorporating spiritual and ethical leadership principles emphasizes the importance of integrity, humility, and a service-oriented approach in building enduring relationships.

CHAPTER 1
What is Symbiosis?

Chapter 1: What is Symbiosis?

The term "symbiosis" originates from the Greek words "syn " (together) and "biosis " (life), describing a relationship in which two or more entities coexist in a mutually beneficial arrangement. While symbiosis is most commonly associated with the biological world, where organisms depend on one another for survival and growth, the concept extends far beyond nature. Symbiosis provides a powerful framework for understanding human relationships, leadership dynamics, and the interconnectedness that defines our universe. Whether in family, friendships, professional settings, or spiritual communities, symbiotic relationships flourish when built on trust, reciprocity, and mutual growth.

This chapter examines the historical roots of symbiosis, contrasts it with relationships that counter its principles, and highlights the advantages of nurturing symbiotic connections across various domains. It also analyzes examples from nature and the universe to demonstrate how symbiosis is a foundational concept interwoven into the fabric of existence. Finally, the chapter concludes by emphasizing the importance of reciprocity and mutual growth as crucial elements in maintaining healthy relationships.

1.1 The Timeless Power of Symbiosis

While the concept of symbiosis originated in biology, its significance extends far beyond the natural world. Introduced by Anton de Bary in 1879, it describes interactions that benefit both parties. Its fundamental principles are evident throughout human history in personal relationships, business partnerships, and international alliances. Over the years, individuals, organizations, and nations have collaborated, leveraging their unique strengths to achieve common goals that would be unattainable individually.

Symbiotic relationships, including thriving business alliances, lasting marriages, and significant global coalitions, have shaped history and still offer essential insights for building meaningful, mutually beneficial connections today. These relationships' successes highlight the power of collaboration, the significance of shared goals, and the strength that arises from interdependence.

While originating from biology, symbiosis reflects human relationships in various fields, including personal, professional, and geopolitical contexts. History shows that collaboration frequently leads to success, highlighting how different entities can come together, amplify their strengths, and reach significantly more impressive results collectively rather than alone. These symbiotic relationships illustrate that the intersection of talents, resources, and visions fosters an environment ripe for growth, stability, and innovation.

In the corporate world, symbiotic relationships are exemplified in various forms of collaboration, including strategic alliances, joint ventures, and partnerships. These arrangements enable organizations to pool their resources and expertise, allowing them to pursue shared goals more effectively than they could independently. By combining complementary strengths in technology, market access, or specialized knowledge, companies can drive innovation and create new products or services that meet evolving consumer demands.

Such collaborations often result in significant market expansions, enabling entities to explore new territories or demographics that would otherwise be difficult to penetrate. Furthermore, these partnerships can strengthen competitive advantages by sharing the risks and costs related to research and development, marketing, and infrastructure investments. Overall, the interplay of these relationships fosters a spirit of collaboration, contributing to a more dynamic and adaptive business ecosystem.

Symbiosis is evident in personal relationships, where lasting friendships, marriages, and partnerships thrive on mutual respect, trust, and shared values. These core elements cultivate an environment that nurtures emotional security, resilience, and personal growth. In these relationships, individuals can communicate openly and provide mutual support, fostering vulnerability and genuine expression. Just as organisms in nature flourish through interdependence, humans gain strength and well-being from supportive partnerships. This interconnectedness boosts individual self-esteem and enhances social interactions, fostering a more profound sense of community and belonging. Ultimately, these connections empower individuals to tackle life's challenges more effectively, navigating experiences with the assurance of dependable support, much like ecosystems where every component contributes to the overall health of the whole.

Symbiosis, in all its forms, offers a timeless framework for understanding how collaboration and interdependence can drive success across multiple spheres. In business, it fosters innovation and growth. In personal relationships, it nurtures emotional security and mutual flourishing. On a global scale, it promotes peace and collective progress. The essence of symbiosis encourages us to embrace interdependence, leverage complementary strengths, and pursue shared goals.

As we navigate an increasingly complex and interconnected world, the principles of symbiosis remain a guiding light. They remind us that by collaborating, we can achieve more, foster stronger relationships, and create a more harmonious existence. Whether in the marketplace, the home, or the global community, symbiosis offers a pathway to sustainable success, resilience, and transformative impact.

1.1.1 Symbiosis in Successful Business Partnerships

Many of the most successful companies and brands have emerged from symbiotic partnerships characterized by a harmonious blend of complementary skills, knowledge, and resources. These collaborations often thrived not because the partners shared identical traits or visions, but because they strategically leveraged their diverse strengths. By combining various areas of expertise, such as technology, marketing, finance, and design, the partners created innovative solutions and products that held greater value than any of their contributions could achieve alone.

For instance, when brainstorming new ideas, one partner might excel in creative thinking, while another might possess strong analytical skills, enabling them to evaluate the feasibility of these concepts. Similarly, one organization may provide a robust distribution network, while the other offers cutting-edge technology. Together, they can address market challenges more effectively and seize new opportunities, demonstrating that the combination of diverse perspectives and strengths often drives significant breakthroughs in business. This principle of collaboration highlights the notion that effective partnerships can result in extraordinary outcomes and lasting impacts in the marketplace.

1. Apple: Steve Jobs and Steve Wozniak

Few business partnerships demonstrate the impact of mutual gain as distinctly as the collaboration between Steve Jobs and Steve Wozniak, the co-founders of Apple Inc. Their teamwork exemplified a harmonious blend of vision and execution. Jobs contributed his innovative marketing acumen and forward-thinking mindset, while Wozniak brought extraordinary technical expertise and engineering innovation. Wozniak was the intellectual force behind creating the inaugural Apple computer, the Apple I, which he meticulously developed in his garage. This endeavor showcased his remarkable proficiency in hardware design, paving the way for future technological advancements. At the same time, Jobs leveraged his extensive knowledge of market trends and user experience to convert Wozniak's technical accomplishments into commercially successful products. His influence was crucial in developing strategies for showcasing Apple's offerings, ensuring they resonated with consumers in a rapidly evolving tech landscape.

Their combined strengths transformed the tech industry, leading to innovative products that changed personal computing. This collaboration created a lasting company and established Apple as one of the world's most prominent and influential brands. Together, they revolutionized how people interact with technology and paved the way for a new digital innovation and creativity era.

☑ **Symbiotic Dynamics:**

- **Complementary Strengths:** Wozniak's technical brilliance and Jobs' strategic vision.

- **Shared Purpose:** A mission to make computing accessible to everyday people.
- **Mutual Growth:** Their partnership resulted in the development of revolutionary technologies that reshaped entire industries.

2. Disney and Pixar: Merging Creativity with Technology

A notable case of symbiosis in business is the strategic partnership between Disney and Pixar. Pixar, renowned for its state-of-the-art animation technology and creative storytelling, collaborated with Disney, which is known for its rich storytelling legacy and vast global distribution network. This alliance proved highly successful, resulting in a series of revolutionary animated films, including classics like Toy Story, the first feature-length movie created entirely with computer-generated imagery, and Finding Nemo, which enchanted viewers with its touching narrative and breathtaking visuals. The partnership redefined animated storytelling and established new benchmarks for the animation industry. The successful release of these films signaled the beginning of a new era, demonstrating that animated movies could earn both critical and commercial success.

In 2006, Disney strengthened its partnership with Pixar by acquiring the company for an estimated $7.4 billion. This deal ensured access to Pixar's innovative technology and creative talent while enabling both organizations to leverage their distinct advantages: Disney's unrivaled storytelling ability and Pixar's animation expertise, to create an extraordinary collection of cinematic works that still resonate with global audiences. Together, they have captivated millions and transformed the animated film industry, inspiring numerous creators.

☑ **Symbiotic Dynamics:**

- **Creative Synergy:** Pixar's technical innovation complemented Disney's storytelling expertise.

- **Mutual Benefit:** Disney gained technological prowess, while Pixar accessed a broader platform to showcase its creativity.

- **Long-Term Growth:** The partnership produced consistent box office success and enhanced both brands.

3. Procter & Gamble and Walmart: Supply Chain Efficiency

The strategic partnership between Procter & Gamble (P&G) and Walmart demonstrates the powerful concept of supply chain symbiosis, where both companies thrive through collaboration. By exchanging real-time data and maintaining seamless communication, P&G has ensured that Walmart's shelves are consistently stocked with a diverse range of popular products. This proactive approach ensures that consumers consistently find what they seek and enables Walmart to reduce its inventory costs significantly. As a result, Walmart has improved its supply chain management, enhancing efficiency and profitability for retailers and manufacturers alike.

☑ **Symbiotic Dynamics:**

- **Operational Alignment:** P&G's manufacturing strength met Walmart's logistical expertise.

- **Efficiency and Growth:** Both companies gained a competitive edge by streamlining operations.

- **Sustained Success:** The relationship helped both organizations dominate their respective markets.

1.1.2 Symbiosis in Historical Marriages and Relationships

As a covenantal relationship, marriage is one of the most profound illustrations of symbiosis. Strong marriages thrive when spouses bring complementary qualities to the relationship, fostering mutual growth, emotional support, and spiritual edification. Scripture highlights the importance of symbiotic relationships within marriage, emphasizing partnership, commitment, and sacrificial love.

Franklin and Eleanor Roosevelt: Political and Social Partnership

Franklin D. Roosevelt and Eleanor Roosevelt exemplified a unique and dynamic partnership that transcended the conventional boundaries of marriage and political collaboration. As the 32nd President of the United States, Franklin played a crucial role during a time of great national crisis, steering the country through the Great Depression and World War II. Meanwhile, Eleanor emerged as a powerful advocate for human rights, women's rights, and social justice, utilizing her platform to highlight issues that often went unnoticed.

Their relationship was marked by mutual respect and collaboration, with Eleanor playing a crucial role in shaping domestic policies and advocating for humanitarian causes. She traveled extensively, delivering speeches and engaging with marginalized communities, which gave her firsthand insight into the struggles faced by ordinary Americans. Her activism played a pivotal role in influencing key legislation, including initiatives aimed at improving labor conditions and expanding social services.

Together, the collaborative efforts of Franklin and Eleanor Roosevelt not only transformed the traditional role of the First Lady but also created a powerful example of how a formidable partnership can shape the political landscape. Their unwavering dedication to social reform and civic engagement paved the way for significant progress and championed the rights of marginalized communities. Through their advocacy, they forged a lasting legacy that resonates through time, inspiring future generations to pursue justice and equality in their own communities.

Symbiotic Dynamics:

- **Political Influence:** Franklin's leadership was amplified by Eleanor's advocacy.
- **Mutual Empowerment:** Both contributed to shaping American history.
- **Lasting Legacy:** Their partnership profoundly influenced civil rights and global diplomacy.

1.1.3 Symbiosis in International Alliances

Historically, nations have built alliances based on mutual benefit, characterized by commitments to defense, resource sharing, and strategic advantage that strengthen both parties. These collaborations often act as significant catalysts for political stability, creating conditions where governance can prosper. Moreover, they have promoted economic development, allowing countries to access new markets and boost trade opportunities. Such partnerships have not only increased their collective global influence but have also influenced the trajectory of history, highlighting the significant impact of cooperation in addressing shared challenges.

1. The United States and the United Kingdom: WWII Partnership

During World War II, the alliance between the United States and the United Kingdom exemplified a profound form of international symbiosis that was instrumental in shaping the course of the conflict. The United States emerged as a powerhouse of industrial resources, leveraging its vast manufacturing capabilities to produce war materials on an unprecedented scale. This included everything from tanks and aircraft to naval ships, with innovations in production techniques like the assembly line dramatically speeding up output. Along with this industrial might, the U.S. also brought significant technological advancements, such as radar systems, code-breaking capabilities, and the development of the atomic bomb.

Conversely, the United Kingdom played a crucial role by contributing military strategy and operational experience acquired from its extensive colonial engagements. The U.K.'s intelligence community, particularly through initiatives like codebreaking at Bletchley Park, supplied essential insights into enemy plans, enabling the Allies to anticipate and counter Axis strategies. Furthermore, Britain's profound understanding of European geopolitics and regional dynamics proved invaluable in maintaining unity among the diverse Allied forces.

Together, the United States and the United Kingdom coordinated their efforts to lead the Allied forces to a decisive victory over the Axis powers. This collaboration not only resulted in military success but also laid the groundwork for a transformed global political landscape, fostering a post-war order that aimed to prevent future conflicts through institutions like the United Nations and by deepening transatlantic relations. The alliance served as a testament to the power of cooperation, demonstrating how nations can achieve remarkable outcomes when they effectively combine their respective strengths toward a common goal.

☑ **Symbiotic Dynamics:**

- **Strategic Collaboration:** Military strength combined with tactical expertise.
- **Shared Resources:** Leveraging industrial and logistical power.
- **Global Impact:** Their partnership established the foundation for the post-war world order.

2. Japan and South Korea: Economic Cooperation

Despite a history of conflict and tension, Japan and South Korea have increasingly forged a symbiotic economic relationship over the past few decades. This partnership is largely driven by Japan's cutting-edge technology and South Korea's strong manufacturing capabilities. Together, they have created a synergy that has resulted in substantial mutual economic growth and remarkable technological advancements.

The collaboration between these two nations has enhanced their global competitiveness, particularly in vital sectors such as electronics and automotive manufacturing. Japan's innovations in areas like semiconductors and robotics enhance South Korea's strengths in mass production and assembly, promoting the creation of highly sophisticated products. This interaction not only boosts the economies of both countries but also establishes them as key players in the global supply chain.

Moreover, collaborative efforts such as joint research and development projects and strategic investments have greatly strengthened the economic ties between Japan and South Korea. This partnership enables both nations to tackle shared challenges, ranging from technological innovation to sustainable development, while simultaneously exploring new avenues for growth and opportunity. As a result, Japan and South Korea are not only nurturing their own economic prosperity but also playing a crucial role in shaping the dynamics of global trade and setting standards for emerging technologies worldwide.

Symbiotic Dynamics:

- **Technological Exchange:** Sharing expertise for mutual industrial advancement.
- **Economic Growth:** Increased competitiveness in global markets.
- **Strategic Stability:** Strengthening regional influence and security.

3. NATO: Collective Security and Defense

The North Atlantic Treaty Organization (NATO) exemplifies a significant instance of symbiosis within the realm of international relations, embodying the principles of collective security among its member states. Established in the wake of World War II, NATO operates as a military alliance wherein member nations collaborate closely to bolster their defense capabilities. Each member contributes an array of military assets, including personnel, advanced weaponry, and strategic intelligence, thereby fostering a resilient network of mutual support and shared resources.

This collaborative approach not only enhances individual nations' security but also is a significant deterrent against potential external threats. By pledging to collective defense, as articulated in Article 5 of the NATO treaty, member states affirm that an attack on one is regarded as an attack on all, thereby reinforcing their collective resolve. Through systematic joint exercises, intelligence sharing, and strategic planning, NATO fosters a dynamic environment of cooperation, adaptability, and trust, which is crucial for addressing the intricate security challenges of the contemporary world.

☑ **Symbiotic Dynamics:**

- **Mutual Defense:** An attack on one is treated as an attack on all.
- **Resource Sharing:** Leveraging technological and military assets.
- **Global Stability:** Maintaining peace and order through collective strength.

Conclusion: The Timeless Power of Symbiosis

From boardrooms to battlefields and marriage covenants to international diplomacy, the concept of symbiosis has emerged as a timeless and transformative force across various spheres of life. This relationship between two entities, whether individuals or groups, can yield remarkable outcomes when they align their strengths, pursue common objectives, and maintain accountability to one another. Such collaboration fosters an environment conducive to innovation, resilience, and sustained growth.

As we delve deeper into subsequent chapters, continued examples of symbiosis will provide a rich foundation for applying a new relationship theory to both personal and professional relationships. Peering into the past, we can reflect on history and observe how effective alliances and collaborations have overcome challenges, leading to enduring relationships. These partnerships cultivate growth and facilitate meaningful positive change in our communities.

1.2 The Counter to Symbiosis

Symbiosis, characterized by mutual benefit and shared growth, fosters stability and cooperation among individuals, organizations, or nations. In contrast, its antithesis surfaces in relationships marked by exploitation, manipulation, and deep-seated imbalance. While these dysfunctional relationships may initially present an illusion of functionality, they gradually erode the foundational trust necessary for any meaningful connection. Over time, the corrosive effects of exploitation diminish the inherent value within these interactions, ultimately leading to stagnation or even complete collapse.

The primary threats to symbiotic relationships include parasitism, exploitation, and unchecked competition. Parasitism, where one party gains at the expense of another, can destabilize interactions by creating resentment and dependency. Exploitation, driven by power imbalances, undermines equitable exchange, sowing the seeds of conflict. Unchecked competition, while sometimes fostering innovation, can escalate to harmful levels, leading to aggressive behaviors that prioritize individual success over collective well-being. Each of these dangers poses a significant risk to the health and sustainability of relationships, underscoring the importance of cultivating symbiotic connections that promote collaboration and mutual respect.

This section explores the counterforces undermining healthy relationships, highlighting their destructive consequences through historical examples, notable business failures, and personal relational breakdowns. For instance, the downfall of successful companies often arises from toxic leadership behavior characterized by self-serving decisions disregarding the welfare of employees and stakeholders. Similarly, personal relationships can deteriorate when one party prioritizes their ambitions over trust and collaboration.

By examining these threats in detail, we can better equip leaders and individuals to recognize the early signs of parasitism. Proactively addressing these issues is crucial; failing to do so can lead to irreversible damage, affecting individual relationships and broader organizational and community well-being. Understanding the nuances of these destructive patterns enables us to cultivate healthier interactions and foster environments where respect and humility thrive.

1.2.1 Parasitism: The One-Sided Relationship

Parasitism occurs in nature when one organism benefits at the expense of another, often by depleting essential resources without providing any reciprocal benefits. This behavior can also manifest in human relationships, where one individual takes advantage of another, gaining value while not contributing to mutual growth or success. Such parasitic relationships, whether occurring on a personal, professional, or organizational level, can lead to significant imbalances, eroding trust and depleting the host's resources over time. As the parasitic party continues to take without giving, the strength and well-being of the host diminish, ultimately destabilizing the relationship and often resulting in its collapse. This destructive pattern underscores the importance of mutual support and collaboration, which are essential for healthy, thriving connections, whether among individuals or within organizations.

Parasitic Relationships in Business: Enron's Deception

The collapse of Enron Corporation remains one of the most infamous examples of parasitism in the business world. Once celebrated as a shining star on Wall Street, Enron's rapid decline was primarily fueled by unethical accounting practices designed to inflate profits exaggeratedly while cleverly obscuring significant debt. Executives at Enron employed deceitful tactics, such as mark-to-market accounting, allowing them to record potential future profits as current income. This manipulation not only misled stakeholders about the company's actual financial health but also created a disguise of strong growth that attracted investors and inflated stock prices.

Moreover, executives exploited employees by promoting an aggressive corporate culture that rewarded short-term gains over long-term stability. Many employees invested their retirement savings in Enron stock, believing in the company's misleading success. As the truth unraveled, thousands lost their jobs and savings while top executives reaped millions in bonuses just before the company's demise. Ultimately, Enron's deceptive practices siphoned billions of dollars from its resources, leading to one of the largest bankruptcies in American history and shaking public trust in corporate governance and accounting practices. The scandal was a cautionary tale about the dangers of prioritizing profit over ethics, highlighting the need for greater accountability within corporate structures.

☑ **Parasitic Dynamics:**

- **Exploitation of Trust:** Investors relied on misleading information.
- **Depletion of Resources:** Employees and shareholders suffered irreparable losses.
- **Collapse of the Host:** Enron's downfall left thousands unemployed and devastated financial markets.

Parasitism in Personal Relationships: Emotional and Financial Drain

In personal relationships, parasitic behavior can emerge in different, often subtle ways. These relationships may include friendships, family connections, or romantic partnerships. At the heart of parasitic behavior lies an imbalance, where one individual consistently takes while the other continuously gives, leading to significant emotional consequences.

In friendships, for instance, a one-sided relationship may involve one friend consistently relying on the other for support without offering anything in return. This can lead to feelings of resentment over time, as the supportive friend may feel taken for granted and undervalued. In romantic relationships, emotional or financial parasitism can develop when one partner depends heavily on the other for emotional stability or financial security, often resulting in feelings of powerlessness or dissatisfaction for the given partner.

Family relationships can also be breeding grounds for these patterns. It can become commonplace for certain family members to depend on others for emotional or financial support, creating an environment where some feel burdened while others feel entitled. This imbalance can erode familial bonds and lead to long-lasting fractures. Recognizing the signs of parasitic behavior is essential for maintaining healthy relationships. Key indicators include feelings of exhaustion, resentment, and a persistent sense of obligation without appreciation. Over time, these relationships can drain one's self-esteem and happiness, leading to isolation and a sense of being trapped in a cycle of giving without receiving.

To address these issues, open communication is essential. Establishing clear boundaries and expressing needs can help restore balance, enabling both parties to contribute meaningfully to the relationship. Sometimes, it may be necessary to reevaluate the relationship entirely, particularly if efforts to restore balance are continually met with resistance or denial. Fostering healthy relationships requires a mutual understanding of each other's needs and a commitment to supporting one another, cultivating a rewarding and fulfilling partnership for both parties. Recognizing and addressing parasitic behavior is crucial for cultivating healthier, more equitable connections in our lives.

Signs of Parasitic Personal Relationships:

- **Unreciprocated Effort:** One person constantly gives while the other takes.
- **Emotional Manipulation:** The taker uses guilt or coercion to maintain control.

- **Lack of Accountability:** The relationship lacks mutual investment and growth.

1.2.2 Exploitation: Manipulating for Personal Gain

Exploitation refers to a situation where one party systematically manipulates another for personal gain, often using tactics such as deceit, coercion, or emotional manipulation. Unlike parasitism, which may occur unconsciously or develop gradually, exploitation is characterized by intentional, calculated actions to benefit one individual at the direct expense of another.

This relational dysfunction is frequently rooted in significant power imbalances, with one party holding greater influence or control, enabling them to take advantage of the vulnerable position of the other. Factors like greed, a lack of ethical boundaries, and the desire for dominance typically fuel such behavior. The implications of exploitation can be profound, resulting in emotional, psychological, and even financial harm for the exploited party, while perpetuating cycles of inequality and distress within relationships and communities.

Exploitation in Leadership: The Downfall of Theranos

Theranos, a high-profile biotech startup founded by Elizabeth Holmes in 2003, serves as a cautionary tale of exploitation and misguided leadership within the technology sector. Holmes, depicted as a visionary entrepreneur, claimed that her company had developed revolutionary blood-testing technology capable of conducting a myriad of tests using just a few drops of blood. This extravagant promise captivated the attention of investors, employees, and the media, who were eager for breakthroughs in healthcare innovation.

Holmes skillfully harnessed this enthusiasm by promoting her vision, often enhancing the capabilities of the technology and the company's progress. Consequently, Theranos attracted nearly $1 billion in investment from prominent backers, including venture capitalists and influential figures in business and politics. The promise of making healthcare more accessible and affordable resonated with a society increasingly impatient for medical advancements.

However, behind the facade of success lay a complex web of deceit. Investigative reports revealed that the technology was not only unproven but also fundamentally flawed. As scrutiny mounted, the truth began to surface, leading to a series of legal battles and public outcry. Ultimately, Theranos crumbled under the weight of its lies, resulting in significant financial losses for investors and irrevocable damage to public trust in health startups. This downfall not only highlighted the dangers of unchecked ambition and manipulation in leadership but also served as a reminder of the ethical responsibility that accompanies innovation in the healthcare industry.

Exploitation Dynamics:

- **Deceptive Practices:** Misleading stakeholders to pursue personal gain.
- **Power Imbalance:** Manipulating others without regard for consequences.
- **Erosion of Trust:** Loss of credibility and destruction of relationships.

Exploitation in International Relations: Colonialism and Resource Control

Colonialism represents a profound and pervasive form of exploitation that has shaped global dynamics throughout history. At its core, colonial powers aimed to dominate and control vast territories, extracting valuable resources such as minerals, agricultural products, and other raw materials from these colonized regions. This extraction often depended on the forced labor of local populations, who faced harsh working conditions and received little to no compensation.

In exchange for these resources, colonial powers typically provided minimal infrastructure development and few social benefits, instead focusing on maximizing their profits. This significant imbalance enriched colonizing nations while leaving deep economic and cultural scars on the colonized societies. The repercussions of this exploitation can still be felt today, as many of these regions continue to struggle with underdevelopment, social inequality, and cultural disintegration. Furthermore, the long-term effects of colonialism often manifested as disrupted social structures and eroded local traditions, contributing to ongoing challenges in addressing historical grievances and fostering sustainable development.

☑ **Exploitation Dynamics:**

- **Resource Extraction:** Colonizers gained wealth while indigenous populations suffered.
- **Cultural Erosion:** Suppression of native traditions and identities.
- **Long-Term Consequences:** Generational economic disparity and social upheaval.

1.2.3 Unchecked Competition: Destroying Relationships Through Rivalry

Competition can act as a powerful catalyst for growth and innovation, motivating individuals and organizations to push boundaries and strive for excellence. However, when competition becomes unchecked, it can create an environment of hostility, mistrust, and division. In such cases, personal, organizational, or international relationships often become defined solely by rivalry. This singular focus on defeating opponents undermines collaboration and mutual benefit, which are crucial for sustainable success.

Moreover, this adversarial mindset gives rise to a form of counter-symbiosis, where instead of working together toward common goals, entities become entrenched in their desire for individual dominance. Over time, this relentless pursuit can erode the foundational elements of trust and relational stability. When trust diminishes, communication falters, and cooperation dwindles, ultimately hindering progress and prosperity for all involved. Therefore, it is crucial to strike a balance between healthy competition and collaborative efforts to foster environments where mutual growth and innovation can thrive.

Unchecked Competition in Business: The Cola Wars

The fierce rivalry between Coca-Cola and Pepsi, often called the Cola Wars, epitomizes the complexities of unchecked competition in the beverage industry. This conflict not only spurred innovations in product development and creative marketing strategies but also resulted in a range of aggressive tactics that blurred ethical lines. Both companies engaged in relentless price wars, cutting costs in desperate attempts to outmaneuver one another for market share.

At the same time, impressive public relations campaigns sought to develop unique brand identities, attracting consumers with assurances of an enhanced product experience. Yet, as both corporations narrowed their focus on brand dominance, they often neglected the consequences for customer satisfaction. The competitive drive frequently eclipsed the significance of quality and customer loyalty, resulting in a situation where strategies to attract consumers sometimes created a gap between the brands' offerings and actual consumer needs. This competition stands as a cautionary example, highlighting that while rivalry can spur innovation, it may also create a fragmented market that values corporate achievement over real customer connection.

☑ **Unchecked Competition Dynamics:**

- **Short-Term Gains, Long-Term Losses:** Price wars eroded profitability.
- **Brand Polarization:** Loyalty to one brand at the expense of constructive innovation.
- **Market Saturation:** An oversaturated market where differentiation became increasingly difficult.

Unchecked Competition in Politics: Athens & Sparta – The Peloponnesian War

The longstanding rivalry between Athens and Sparta, culminating in the devastating conflict known as the Peloponnesian War (431–404 BC), exemplifies how unchecked competition can lead to catastrophic outcomes on a geopolitical scale. Driven by a fierce desire for supremacy, both city-states became embroiled in a protracted conflict that not only depleted their military and economic resources but also profoundly affected their social structures.

Athens, with its powerful navy and democratic ideals, sought to expand its influence across the Aegean, while Sparta, recognized for its formidable land army and oligarchic governance, aimed to assert its dominance over the Peloponnesian peninsula. This deep-seated animosity was intensified by various alliances and betrayals, including the formation of the Delian League by Athens and the Peloponnesian League led by Sparta.

As the war dragged on for nearly three decades, the toll on both populations was immense, with countless lives lost in battles and widespread famine plaguing the regions. The strain of continuous conflict weakened their collective military capacities and civil morale, rendering both city-states vulnerable to external threats. The eventual defeat of Athens not only marked the decline of Athenian democracy but also ushered in a period of instability that allowed for foreign invasions, including the rise of Macedonian power under Philip II. Thus, the Peloponnesian War exemplifies how intense rivalry and ambition, when left unchecked, can lead to self-destruction and destabilization across an entire region.

☑ Unchecked Competition Dynamics:

- **Erosion of Diplomacy:** Failure to seek peaceful resolutions.
- **Mutual Destruction:** Prolonged conflict weakened both states.

- **Loss of Influence:** Both Athens and Sparta emerged weakened and vulnerable to external powers.

1.2.4 The Consequences of Counter-Symbiotic Relationships

When relationships deteriorate into patterns of parasitism, exploitation, or unrestrained competition, the repercussions extend far beyond immediate interactions and often lead to lasting harm. In such counter-symbiotic situations, the foundational elements of trust begin to erode, creating a toxic environment where collaboration is replaced by self-interest. Whether emotional, financial, or environmental, resources become overexploited and depleted, leaving little room for recovery or growth. This relentless pursuit of short-term gains often blinds individuals or groups to the long-term consequences of their actions, ultimately sacrificing the stability and health of the relationship for fleeting benefits. As the fabric of trust unravels, the potential for meaningful partnerships diminishes, leading to a cycle of conflict and dissatisfaction that can be incredibly challenging to reverse.

Relational Breakdown

- Emotional exhaustion and disillusionment.
- Breakdown of trust and mutual respect.

Organizational Collapse

- Loss of stakeholder confidence.
- Financial instability and reputational damage.

Geopolitical Instability

- Long-term economic and social repercussions.
- Increased vulnerability to external threats.

Conclusion: Guarding Against Counter-Symbiosis

Understanding the destructive forces hindering symbiosis is crucial for leaders, individuals, and organizations. This awareness allows individuals to identify and address unhealthy relationship patterns before they take root. Establishing an environment that highlights mutual benefit is essential in various situations, whether in personal relationships, business partnerships, or international diplomacy.

This involves creating shared accountability and promoting ethical conduct as a foundational principle. By doing so, stakeholders can build trust and cooperation, which are vital for sustaining symbiotic relationships. Leaders should actively encourage open communication and transparency, ensuring that all parties feel valued and heard. Furthermore, cultivating a culture of respect and empathy can significantly enhance collaboration, making it easier to navigate conflicts and challenges that may arise. A commitment to these principles is key to nurturing enduring, productive relationships that can adapt and thrive over time.

As we advance to examine 1.3 The Benefits of a Symbiotic Relationship, we will investigate how aligning relationships with symbiotic principles fosters environments where trust, growth, and long-term success thrive.

1.3 The Benefits of a Symbiotic Relationship

Symbiotic relationships, defined by intentionality and a spirit of reciprocity, yield significant benefits in both personal and professional contexts. These relationships foster environments that promote mutual growth, enhance trust, and support sustained stability. By prioritizing symbiosis, individuals and organizations can nurture a collaborative atmosphere where shared goals are pursued and celebrated.

Each party brings unique strengths and perspectives in such settings, fostering innovative solutions and enhancing creativity. This collaboration deepens connections and establishes a resilient framework capable of adapting to challenges and opportunities. The long-term benefits of nurturing these relationships, such as increased loyalty, shared resources, and expanded networks, often far exceed what each party could accomplish alone. Investing in symbiotic relationships transforms interactions into thriving partnerships that benefit everyone involved.

1.3.1 Mutual Growth and Development

At the core of symbiosis lies the fundamental principle of mutual growth, where both parties actively invest in one another's success. This reciprocal relationship fosters an environment of continuous improvement and development, enabling both individuals and organizations to thrive together. In these connections, each party's strengths are amplified and acknowledged, while vulnerabilities are identified and addressed, leading to a more resilient partnership. As a result, both entities experience transformative growth, harnessing their combined capabilities to innovate, adapt, and overcome challenges. Ultimately, these vibrant interactions foster a flourishing environment where teamwork facilitates advancement and cultivates enduring relationships.

Mutual Growth in Business: Microsoft and Intel

The enduring partnership between Microsoft and Intel, commonly known as the Wintel Alliance, is a prime example of how collaborative synergy can foster innovation and stimulate growth in the technology sector. Since the early days of personal computing, Microsoft's software, particularly its Windows operating systems, has been intricately designed to leverage Intel's processors' capabilities. In turn, Intel's cutting-edge hardware has consistently pushed the boundaries of performance, enabling Microsoft's software to run more efficiently and effectively.

This symbiotic relationship has not only empowered both companies to dominate the personal computing market for several decades but has also played a pivotal role in shaping the technological landscape we know today. By aligning their strategies and investments, Microsoft and Intel have driven significant advancements in computing power, user interface design, and overall functionality, leading to widespread market penetration and consumer adoption.

Together, they have effectively navigated the rapidly evolving tech industry by adapting to emerging trends and challenges. This collaboration demonstrates how two industry leaders can leverage each other's strengths to drive innovation. They have established a strong ecosystem that advances technological progress.

Mutual Growth Dynamics:

- **Complementary Expertise:** Microsoft's software innovation complemented Intel's hardware capabilities.
- **Co-evolution:** Both companies adapted and improved their products based on shared insights.
- **Market Expansion:** Their partnership propelled the PC revolution, benefiting consumers and reshaping technology.

Mutual Growth in Mentorship: Warren Buffett and Bill Gates

The relationship between Warren Buffett, widely regarded as one of the most successful investors of all time, and Bill Gates, the co-founder of Microsoft, stands as a powerful example of how mutual growth flourishes through mentorship. Their friendship began in the mid-1990s, strengthened by a shared passion for learning and a commitment to positively impacting the world.

Buffett, renowned for his sharp insights into value investing and his ability to anticipate market trends, imparted his extensive knowledge of philanthropy and business strategy to Gates. This guidance greatly impacted Gates's approach to charitable giving, assisting him in refining his vision for meaningful philanthropy. In turn, Gates exposed Buffett to the transformative power of technology and innovation, broadening Buffett's understanding of the fast-changing digital landscape.

Their collaborative efforts led to the establishment of the Bill & Melinda Gates Foundation in 2000, which has since developed into one of the largest and most influential philanthropic organizations worldwide. The foundation focuses on various initiatives, including global health, education, and poverty alleviation, reflecting both leaders' commitment to addressing some of the world's most pressing challenges. This symbiotic relationship highlights the significance of mentorship in personal and professional growth and emphasizes the potential for visionary leaders to enhance their impact by combining their unique strengths and insights.

Mutual Growth Dynamics:

- **Knowledge Exchange:** Sharing expertise in investing and technology.
- **Philanthropic Impact:** Leveraging resources to address global challenges.
- **Sustained Influence:** Their partnership amplified their individual contributions to society.

1.3.2 Increased Trust and Emotional Security

Trust is the cornerstone of all symbiotic relationships between individuals or organizations. Trust is established and cultivated over time by deliberately prioritizing transparency, integrity, and consistency. In environments where trust is prominent, participants feel a heightened sense of emotional security and psychological safety. This atmosphere encourages individuals to take risks, share their vulnerabilities, and engage in meaningful contributions without fear of judgment or repercussion.

When organizations foster trust, they cultivate a culture where open communication is the norm and collaboration flourishes. Team members feel empowered to express their ideas and concerns and feel confident that their contributions are valued and respected. This collective sense of safety promotes innovation, as individuals are more inclined to propose creative solutions and explore uncharted territories when they believe their peers support them.

Furthermore, building trust enhances resilience in relationships. Although challenges and conflicts are inevitable, a trusting environment inspires individuals to address disagreements in a constructive manner. They approach issues with the understanding that their commitment to one another surpasses temporary setbacks. Ultimately, this trust fosters deeper connections, increased loyalty, and a shared vision, all of which are essential for any relationship or organization's lasting success and sustainability.

Building Trust in Business: Southwest Airlines' Culture of Trust

Southwest Airlines has established a formidable reputation in the aviation industry, primarily due to its strong customer-centric culture and commitment to operational excellence. The deep trust cultivated among management, employees, and customers is central to the airline's success. This trust is nurtured by empowering employees to make informed decisions at all levels of the organization, which not only enhances job satisfaction but also fosters a sense of ownership and accountability.

Additionally, Southwest Airlines stresses transparency in its communication practices. The airline ensures that every team member aligns with its core values and goals by maintaining open communication between management and staff. This transparency also extends to customer interactions, emphasizing honesty and clarity, which fosters stronger relationships with passengers.

The results of this culture are impressive: Southwest consistently outperforms its competitors in key performance indicators, including customer satisfaction ratings, employee loyalty metrics, and overall profitability. This approach not only fosters a positive atmosphere within the company but also leads to exceptional service for customers, creating a loyal customer base that chooses Southwest Airlines time and again.

☑ **Trust Dynamics:**

- **Employee Empowerment:** Encouraging autonomy and decision-making.
- **Open Communication:** Fostering transparency and mutual respect.
- **Customer Loyalty:** Building trust through consistent service and reliability.

1.3.3 Sustainable Stability and Resilience

Symbiotic relationships form a crucial foundation for achieving sustainable stability by fostering balance, adaptability, and resilience. In both organizations and interpersonal connections, these mutually beneficial partnerships enable individuals and groups to navigate challenges more effectively. The fundamental nature of symbiosis is marked by mutual reliance and common goals, enhancing the connections among participants.

As a result, organizations founded on symbiotic principles are better equipped to face adversity since they can draw on collective resources and skills. This collaborative approach fosters resilience, enabling members to adapt to changing circumstances more readily. Moreover, these relationships are crucial in reinforcing long-term commitment, as each party understands the value they provide to one another. By prioritizing cooperative growth and interdependence, these symbiotic connections not only thrive during stable times but also emerge stronger during crises.

Stability in Global Alliances: NATO's Collective Security

The North Atlantic Treaty Organization (NATO) exemplifies the interconnectedness present in international relations, particularly through its commitment to collective security and mutual defense. Founded in 1949, NATO consists of member countries that agree to defend one another against aggression, thereby promoting stability and resilience in a diverse global environment filled with various external threats. Central to NATO's effectiveness is the principle of collective defense articulated in Article 5 of the North Atlantic Treaty, which states that an attack on one member is considered an attack on all. This mutual commitment not only enhances the security of each nation but also fosters a sense of shared responsibility among members, strengthening their relationships and collective capabilities.

NATO's success is derived from its capacity to adjust to shifting geopolitical landscapes, transforming from a military alliance aimed at deterring the Soviet Union during the Cold War into a flexible organization that tackles contemporary challenges like terrorism, cyber threats, and regional disputes. The alliance also forges partnerships beyond its member states, fostering dialogue and collaboration with various countries and international organizations. Through joint military exercises, intelligence sharing, and strategic planning, NATO ensures its member nations are prepared and equipped to tackle emerging challenges, thereby contributing to long-term stability in the North Atlantic region and beyond. In this manner, NATO not only protects the security of its members but also serves as a fundamental pillar of international peace and cooperation.

✅ **Stability Dynamics:**

- **Mutual Defense:** Ensuring collective security for all member nations.
- **Resource Sharing:** Pooling military and intelligence resources.
- **Resilience and Adaptability:** Evolving strategies to address global challenges.

1.3.4 Enhanced Creativity and Innovation

Symbiotic relationships enhance creativity and innovation by promoting collaboration and the exchange of diverse ideas. When individuals from various backgrounds and areas of expertise come together, their differing perspectives can spark new insights and approaches, leading to groundbreaking solutions that are challenging to obtain independently. This collaboration fosters a vibrant environment for brainstorming and encourages adaptability, as each participant learns from the experiences and viewpoints of others. As a result, these interactions lay the groundwork for advancements that can transform industries and drive progress in ways that individual efforts often cannot achieve.

Creativity in Business: Google and Android

The partnership between Google and Android revolutionized the mobile sector by launching an open-source operating system that fundamentally altered device functionality and user interaction. Google, as the primary developer, created a powerful platform that laid the groundwork for innovation, while a diverse group of third-party developers contributed significantly by producing a wide array of applications. This collaboration enriched the user experience through inventive and customized apps and greatly expanded Android's market presence. By enabling developers to modify and enhance the operating system, this alliance nurtured a vibrant ecosystem that fostered technological advancement, resulting in a surge of creativity in mobile applications, user interfaces, and features that cater to diverse consumer preferences. As a result, Android gained recognition for its versatility and accessibility in the mobile space, drawing in a diverse range of users and reinforcing its position as a dominant player in the industry.

Innovation Dynamics:

- **Open Ecosystem:** Encouraging external developers to contribute.
- **Shared Vision:** Aligning goals to enhance user experiences.
- **Market Transformation:** Creating a dynamic platform that spurred industry growth.

1.3.5 Legacy and Long-Term Impact

Symbiotic relationships build legacies that extend well beyond those directly involved, leaving lasting impacts on future generations. Such connections within families, businesses, or other interactions often produce advantages that surpass the individuals involved. The benefits of these collaborations, defined by teamwork and mutual support, can influence entire communities and even reshape the course of history.

For example, in a family setting, the values of collaboration and shared responsibility fostered through symbiosis establish a solid groundwork for future generations, influencing their relationships and life decisions. In business, partnerships that embody these principles can drive innovative practices and sustainable growth, creating lasting success that benefits the companies, their employees, and the wider economy. Likewise, in ministry, collaborative efforts can enhance outreach and strengthen community involvement, significantly impacting societal values and spiritual development.

The interaction between relationships creates a lasting legacy that resonates over time, molding cultural values and motivating future leaders and innovators. The strength of collaborative partnerships is in their capability to generate ripples of positive impact that can transcend generations. In essence, these connections play a crucial role in shaping the foundation of our communities.

Legacy in Business: Hewlett-Packard (HP) and Silicon Valley's Culture

The collaboration between Bill Hewlett and Dave Packard played a crucial role in defining the innovation, teamwork, and entrepreneurial spirit associated with Silicon Valley. As the founders of Hewlett-Packard in a garage in 1939, this dynamic duo not only developed groundbreaking technologies but also established a unique business ethos. Their unwavering commitment to ethical leadership nurtured a work environment that prioritized integrity, transparency, and respect for every employee.

Hewlett and Packard championed employee empowerment, believing that allowing workers to express their ideas and contribute would enhance creativity and productivity. This philosophy fostered a strong communal spirit within the organization and encouraged collaboration at every level. Their focus on technological progress and continuous improvement also motivated countless startups and innovators worldwide. Known as the HP Way, their management approach set a benchmark for companies seeking to balance profit with purpose. Their legacy endures today, inspiring entrepreneurs and technology leaders to uphold principles that promote innovation while remaining committed to ethical standards.

Legacy Dynamics:

- **Cultural Influence:** Shaping a model of ethical business practices.
- **Mentorship Impact:** Inspiring future generations of entrepreneurs.
- **Technological Legacy:** Driving innovation in the tech industry.

Conclusion: The Transformative Power of Symbiosis

Symbiotic relationships hold transformative power that can greatly enhance various aspects of life by fostering environments rich in trust, growth, stability, creativity, and legacy. These relationships, whether in business, personal connections, or ministry, are built on fundamental principles of mutual benefit, shared purpose, and accountability. They create a synergy that strengthens individual participants and amplifies collective success.

Symbiosis fundamentally revolves around mutual benefit. When individuals or organizations collaborate toward a common goal, they build accountability that strengthens their commitment to each other. This teamwork boosts productivity and encourages innovation and creativity, as different perspectives come together to create new ideas. To cultivate a symbiotic bond in personal and professional relationships, it's essential to prioritize open communication and empathy. This strategy nurtures a supportive network in which individuals feel valued and secure, leading to deeper connections and more meaningful shared experiences.

Additionally, environments built on trust empower individuals to take calculated risks and be secure in knowing they have their partners' support. This trust is a strong foundation for stability, enabling relationships to withstand challenges and adjust to changing situations. By fostering these interconnected partnerships, individuals and organizations can ultimately realize their full potential, achieving results far beyond what they could attain alone. In this way, symbiotic relationships not only facilitate immediate benefits; they also help forge a legacy where the effects of collaboration resonate over time, inspiring future generations to harness the power of teamwork.

Encouraging cooperation among community members by pursuing common goals and dedicating themselves to service can lead to meaningful outreach and lasting transformation. By collaborating towards a shared mission, participants can cultivate a legacy of positivity and transformation that benefits both themselves and the broader community. Ultimately, by embracing the principles of symbiosis, individuals and organizations unlock their potential to achieve far more collectively than they could ever accomplish individually, paving the way for meaningful and sustainable success.

As we transition to 1.4 Symbiosis in Nature, we will explore how the natural world offers a rich tapestry of symbiotic relationships that reflect and reinforce the principles we aim to apply in human relationships.

1.4 Symbiosis in Nature

Nature showcases some of the most profound and compelling examples of symbiosis, where diverse organisms collaborate, coexist, and thrive through mutually beneficial relationships. These intricate partnerships have evolved over millions of years, demonstrating the remarkable power of interdependence within ecosystems. For instance, in coral reefs, tiny algae and corals work together: the algae provide essential nutrients through photosynthesis, while the corals offer protection and a stable environment. This delicate balance exemplifies the necessity of give-and-take in sustaining life.

Similarly, human connections- whether personal, professional, or spiritual- thrive when they are built on the principles of reciprocity, trust, and shared purpose. Just as ecosystems depend on the intricate interactions of various species to flourish, our relationships benefit from an ongoing exchange of support, understanding, and collaboration. In this way, nurturing healthy, symbiotic relationships in our lives reflects the natural world, emphasizing how cooperation and mutual benefit are essential for growth and fulfillment. By embracing these principles, we can cultivate vibrant communities that mirror the harmonious balance found in nature.

1.4.1 Mutualism: A Blueprint for Win-Win Relationships

Mutualism is a fascinating and widely recognized form of symbiosis, characterized by interactions between two species that provide benefits to both. In these mutually beneficial relationships, each organism plays a vital role, offering something valuable that enhances the partnership. This partnership creates a setting where survival, growth, and reproduction are not just improved, but frequently flourish, as both species cooperate to effectively navigate their ecosystems. Through the sharing of nutrients, defense against predators, or help in sourcing food, mutualism highlights the complex interdependence present in nature.

1. Mycorrhizal Networks: Trees and Fungi in Harmony

One of nature's most intricate examples of mutualism can be seen in the relationship between trees and mycorrhizal fungi. These remarkable fungi create extensive underground networks that intertwine with the roots of trees, forming a symbiotic partnership that enhances their survival and growth. Through these connections, mycorrhizal fungi facilitate the exchange of essential nutrients and water. They significantly increase the surface area of the root system, enabling trees to absorb vital minerals like phosphorus and nitrogen from the soil more efficiently. In return, the trees utilize their capacity for photosynthesis to produce carbohydrates, which serve as a food source for the fungi.

The mutualistic relationship between trees and fungi enhances the health of individual trees and supports the overall ecosystem. This collaboration improves soil structure and fertility while promoting biodiversity. Together, they illustrate the intricate beauty and complexity of ecological interdependence.

☑ Mutualism Dynamics:

- **Nutrient Exchange:** Fungi extend the tree's root system, improving nutrient absorption.
- **Communication Network:** Trees communicate through fungal networks, signaling danger and sharing resources.
- **Resilience and Growth:** Both organisms benefit from enhanced resilience and stability.

Leadership Lesson:

In organizational settings, leaders who actively cultivate ecosystems of knowledge sharing and resource exchange play a pivotal role in creating environments where individuals and teams can flourish. Much like the symbiotic relationship between trees and fungi, where each party enhances the other's growth and resilience, effective leaders prioritize collaboration and innovation by fostering a culture of mutual investment and shared success.

These leaders recognize that when team members openly share their expertise and resources, it enhances both collective problem-solving and interpersonal relationships among colleagues. By creating platforms for open communication and offering opportunities for cross-departmental collaboration, leaders can dismantle silos and promote diverse perspectives.

This approach enhances individual performance and fosters innovation as teams utilize their unique strengths to creatively tackle challenges. By nurturing a supportive and collaborative environment, leaders empower their organizations to adapt and flourish in an ever-evolving landscape. Ultimately, this ensures that every member contributes to and benefits from overall success.

2. Pollination: Bees and Flowers – A Dance of Reciprocity

The relationship between bees and flowering plants exemplifies one of nature's most significant mutualistic partnerships. Bees are drawn to flowers mainly for their nectar, a sugary solution that serves as a vital energy source. In their search for nourishment, bees also gather pollen, which is rich in proteins and essential nutrients necessary for their growth and the development of their young.

As bees move from flower to flower in search of nectar, they inadvertently play a crucial role in the reproductive processes of these plants. Sticky pollen grains adhere to the bees' bodies and are transferred to the stigmas of other blooms, facilitating cross-pollination. This process not only aids in fertilizing flowers but also promotes genetic diversity within plant populations, which is essential for their adaptability and resilience.

The interaction between bees and flowering plants showcases a remarkable balance of benefits: plants improve their reproductive success while bees obtain food resources. This intricate dance of reciprocity ensures the survival of both species and highlights the importance of preserving these relationships within ecosystems. Understanding this symbiotic connection emphasizes pollinators' critical role in maintaining biodiversity and food production, reinforcing the need for conservation efforts to protect these indispensable creatures.

☑ Mutualism Dynamics:

- **Pollination and Reproduction:** Bees enable fertilization while gathering nectar.
- **Sustained Ecosystem:** Pollination supports biodiversity and environmental stability.
- **Reciprocal Benefit:** Both species depend on one another for survival.

Leadership Lesson:

Just as bees and flowers thrive through a mutually beneficial relationship, effective leaders enhance their teams by creating an environment in which every individual's contributions are recognized and valued. These leaders understand that by appreciating each team member's input, they cultivate a sense of belonging and purpose. This atmosphere of reciprocity not only strengthens interpersonal connections but also nurtures loyalty, inspires innovative thinking, and builds trust among team members. When individuals feel their efforts are valued, they are more likely to engage actively, collaborate openly, and contribute creatively to the collective goals, ultimately leading to a more cohesive and high-performing team.

3. Cleaner Fish and Larger Fish: Trust & Service

In coral reef ecosystems, the symbiotic relationship between cleaner fish, cleaner shrimp, and larger fish plays a crucial role in maintaining the health of marine life. Cleaner fish, such as the cleaner wrasse, along with various species of cleaner shrimp, engage in the essential service of removing parasites, dead tissue, and other debris from the skin and gills of larger fish. This process not only provides vital nourishment for the cleaner species but also significantly enhances the well-being of their larger counterparts.

Larger fish, such as groupers and parrotfish, benefit greatly from this interaction as it decreases their vulnerability to diseases and infections that can result from parasitic infestations. By actively seeking out these cleaner organisms, the larger fish demonstrate a remarkable level of trust; they willingly expose themselves to potential threats without retaliating against their tiny helpers. This relationship beautifully exemplifies mutualism, where both parties benefit: the cleaners receive food, while the larger fish enjoy improved health and vitality.

The complexity of this relationship also extends to behavioral cues, as larger fish often utilize specific behavioral signals to attract cleaner species, demonstrating the intricacy of their interactions. This intricate dance of cooperation emphasizes the vital role of trust in their exchanges. Additionally, it highlights the delicate balance within the coral reef ecosystem, where each species contributes to a diverse and thriving underwater community.

Mutualism Dynamics:

- **Risk and Trust:** Larger fish trust the cleaner fish not to exploit their vulnerability.
- **Health and Nourishment:** Cleaner fish gain sustenance while enhancing the well-being of their partners.

- **Sustained Relationship:** The partnership fosters long-term ecological stability.

    Leadership Lesson:

    Trust and service are essential cornerstones of effective leadership and strong relationships. Leaders who actively cultivate environments where trust is prioritized and service is valued create cultures characterized by loyalty, commitment, and continuous growth. By promoting open communication, transparency, and accountability, these leaders encourage their teams to feel secure and appreciated, which in turn inspires them to contribute fully and passionately.

    Just as cleaner fish play a crucial role in the health of larger fish by removing parasites and providing companionship, leaders take on the responsibility of nurturing and safeguarding the well-being of those they lead. They actively listen to their team's needs, provide guidance and support, and empower individuals to develop their skills and achieve their personal and professional goals. This nurturing approach enhances collaboration and innovation while cultivating a sense of belonging, ultimately leading to a thriving, resilient community. In essence, the commitment to trust and service in leadership transforms organizations into environments where every member can flourish and reach their potential.

1.4.2 Commensalism: One Benefits Without Harming the Other

Commensalism is a type of symbiotic relationship where one organism benefits from the interaction, such as gaining food or shelter, while the other organism remains unaffected, neither gaining nor losing. This one-sided benefit illustrates how close proximity and associations among species can create new opportunities for growth, survival, and evolution. For example, epiphytic plants, like orchids, grow on trees, accessing sunlight without harming the host tree. This highlights how some species can thrive in various environments by forming these non-intrusive relationships. Commensalism plays a significant role in ecosystems, demonstrating the intricate networks of life and how diverse interactions contribute to ecological balance.

1. Barnacles and Whales: Piggybacking for Survival

Barnacles are fascinating small crustaceans that provide a compelling example of commensalism- a type of symbiotic relationship in which one organism benefits while the host remains largely unaffected. These creatures adeptly attach themselves to the skin of large marine mammals, particularly whales, forging a connection that, although beneficial for the barnacles, has a minimal impact on the whales. By clinging to their massive hosts, barnacles gain a strategic advantage in their pursuit of sustenance. As the whales navigate vast oceanic waters, they stir up nutrient-rich currents teeming with plankton and other microscopic organisms. This advantageous positioning enables barnacles to effectively filter-feed on these abundant food sources, significantly enhancing their chances of survival and growth in an otherwise competitive marine environment.

The relationship primarily benefits the barnacles; their attachment provides access to a wealth of nutrients that would be difficult to obtain in isolated or less active environments. Meanwhile, the whales, even though they may bear the extra weight of the barnacles, experience little to no detrimental effects on their health or mobility. Their overall well-being and ability to navigate open waters remain largely unchanged despite the presence of these crustaceans. This relationship serves as a striking illustration of how certain species can successfully thrive within unique ecological niches, leveraging the presence of larger organisms like whales without harming their hosts. In this way, barnacles exemplify the complexity of marine ecosystems, where cohabitation can lead to mutual benefits for one party while leaving the other unaffected.

☑ Commensalism Dynamics:

- **Enhanced Survival:** Barnacles gain access to food sources.
- **Minimal Impact:** Whales experience no significant harm.
- **Coexistence:** The relationship sustains both organisms in their respective niches.

Leadership Lesson:

In leadership, commensal relationships often manifest through mentorship and sponsorship models. These connections enable emerging leaders to gain crucial exposure, hands-on experience, and extensive knowledge by engaging closely with established professionals in their fields. Although mentors may not witness immediate benefits from these interactions, their impact is significant and enduring, as they are instrumental in shaping future leaders. By imparting their insights, experiences, and networks, mentors create an environment that fosters growth and innovation, ultimately enhancing the broader success of their industry or organization. This generous act of guidance empowers mentees to navigate their journeys more effectively and cultivates a culture of support and collaboration that benefits everyone involved, establishing a sustainable cycle of leadership development and positive influence.

2. Epiphytic Plants and Host Trees: Living with Minimal Impact

Epiphytes, a captivating group of plants that includes diverse species such as orchids and bromeliads, have evolved to thrive on the branches of larger trees in tropical and subtropical habitats. Unlike parasitic plants, which derive nutrients from their hosts, epiphytes have developed remarkable adaptations that allow them to absorb moisture and essential nutrients directly from the air and rainfall. These adaptations include specialized structures like trichomes and roots that efficiently capture water and nutrients from their surrounding environment. This ability to live high in the canopy enables epiphytes to maximize their access to sunlight, crucial for photosynthesis, and to benefit from increased moisture levels that lower-growing plants may not experience due to competition or shading.

Moreover, epiphytes contribute to the health of their ecosystems by supporting biodiversity. They provide habitats for various small organisms, including insects and birds, which rely on them for shelter and food. This symbiotic relationship enables epiphytes to thrive without negatively impacting the host tree's health, as they do not draw from the tree's resources. Instead, both the epiphytes and the host trees coexist in a delicate balance, enhancing the complexity and resilience of their shared environment. This intricate partnership highlights the fascinating interactions within ecosystems and underscores the importance of preserving these unique relationships.

☑ **Commensalism Dynamics:**

- **Strategic Positioning:** Epiphytes access sunlight and nutrients.
- **Minimal Impact:** Host trees remain unaffected by the presence of epiphytes.
- **Ecosystem Balance:** Commensal relationships contribute to biodiversity.

Leadership Lesson:

Epiphytes serve as a captivating metaphor for the significance of positioning and effectively utilizing existing structures to achieve success in various professional settings. Just as epiphytes flourish by attaching themselves to host plants without extracting nutrients from them, individuals seeking supportive environments and cultivating meaningful mentorship can broaden their knowledge, experience, and opportunities. This symbiotic relationship enables them to enhance their professional growth while ensuring that their advancement does not come at the expense of others. By encouraging collaboration and leveraging available resources, these individuals can navigate their career paths more efficiently, ultimately contributing to a thriving community where everyone benefits.

1.4.3 Parasitism: One Benefits at the Other's Expense

Parasitism contrasts sharply with symbiosis, defining a complex ecological interaction where one organism, called the parasite, gains significant advantages at the expense of another, known as the host. This phenomenon occurs across diverse ecosystems, from forests to oceans, and interestingly, mirrors certain human social interactions. In ecological contexts, parasitic entities like ticks, tapeworms, and specific fungi attach to their hosts primarily to siphon off nutrients and resources. This extraction often inflicts physical damage, degrades health, and reduces vitality in the host, which may present as stunted growth, lower reproductive success, or heightened vulnerability to diseases. For instance, a tick feeding on a mammal's blood not only robs its host of essential nutrients but also risks transmitting ailments like Lyme disease, thereby worsening the harmful impacts of this parasitic relationship.

The consequences of parasitism extend beyond immediate harm to the host. In a broader ecological context, parasites can significantly deplete the host's energy reserves, creating imbalances within the ecosystem. If the parasitic relationship persists unchecked, it may lead to the host's deterioration and possible extinction, which can have cascading effects on other species and the overall health of the ecosystem. For instance, a reduction in a host population caused by severe parasitic infestations can disrupt food chains and change habitat dynamics.

Understanding parasitism enhances our knowledge of these biological interactions and invites a deeper reflection on human relationships. Just as parasites exploit their hosts for survival, similar patterns can emerge in social situations, where one party may manipulate or exploit another for personal gain. This exploitation can lead to serious societal consequences, including inequality, conflict, and a breakdown of trust, highlighting the necessity of recognizing and addressing these factors in our lives and communities. Through this lens, the study of parasitism is a critical reminder of the delicate balance in both natural ecosystems and human relationships.

1. Tapeworms and Hosts: Consuming Vital Resources

One of nature's most well-known examples of parasitism is the relationship between tapeworms and their hosts. Tapeworms are flat, segmented parasites that typically inhabit the intestines of various animals, including humans. They possess specialized structures that enable them to attach firmly to the inner walls of their host's digestive tract, often the small intestine.

Once anchored, tapeworms absorb nutrients directly from their host's digested food, bypassing the need for their digestive systems. They can reach impressive lengths as they grow, sometimes exceeding several feet. This parasitic relationship is detrimental to the host, as tapeworms can significantly deplete essential nutrients such as vitamins and minerals, which leads to malnutrition.

Over time, the host may experience symptoms such as fatigue, weight loss, abdominal pain, and potentially severe health complications if left untreated. In certain cases, heavy infestations can lead to gastrointestinal blockages or infections. The impact of tapeworms underscores the complex and often detrimental nature of parasitic relationships, highlighting the importance of understanding and managing these organisms to safeguard host health.

✅ **Parasitism Dynamics:**

- **Resource Depletion:** Parasites extract the host's energy and nutrients, rendering the host weak and susceptible to illness.

- **Weakened Host:** Hosts might not realize the parasite is present until symptoms are severe, which complicates intervention.
- **Eventual Collapse:** Prolonged parasitic infestations can result in malnourishment, anemia, organ damage, and even death if left untreated.

Leadership Lesson:

In leadership, parasitic relationships can develop within organizations when individuals or departments prioritize their own interests at the expense of their colleagues' well-being and contributions. Likewise, leaders or organizations may exploit employees, draining their energy, creativity, and productivity while neglecting to provide proper support or recognition. Moreover, leaders who micromanage, take credit for team achievements, and manipulate employees for personal gain exhibit behavior akin to a tapeworm, gradually eroding morale, trust, and the organization's vitality.

This self-serving behavior can create a toxic environment where collaboration decreases, leading to increased burnout among team members who feel undervalued and overworked. As a result, overall efficiency declines and morale suffers, hindering the organization's ability to achieve its goals. These parasitic relationships impact personal performance and contribute to higher turnover rates and diminished trust among teams, ultimately harming the organization's culture and productivity. Addressing these challenges involves promoting a culture of mutual support where collective achievements are recognized and individual efforts are valued.

2. Cowbirds and Host Birds: Manipulating for Survival

A compelling example of parasitism in the animal kingdom is demonstrated by cowbirds, particularly through their distinct behavior known as brood parasitism. Unlike most bird species that carefully construct their own nests and raise their young, cowbirds employ a different strategy: they lay their eggs in the nests of other bird species. This clever tactic ensures that the host birds unknowingly take on the responsibility of incubating the cowbird's eggs.

The host birds, often unaware of the deception, invest time and resources into raising these eggs, which can come at the expense of their own offspring. When the cowbird chicks hatch, they frequently display aggressive behaviors that allow them to dominate resources. These chicks grow rapidly and outcompete the host's biological young for food, resulting in tragic outcomes where the host chicks may suffer from malnutrition and even perish due to the lack of parental care directed toward them. This parasitic relationship highlights the intricate and often harsh realities of survival in the natural world, illustrating the lengths to which some species will go to ensure their reproductive success.

Parasitic Dynamics:

- **Exploitation of Host Resources:** Host birds unknowingly invest time and energy into raising the parasitic chick.
- **Manipulation and Deception:** Cowbird eggs mimic the host's eggs, preventing rejection and ensuring incubation.

- **Displacement of Host Offspring:** Cowbird chicks demand disproportionate amounts of food, weakening or eliminating the host's biological offspring.

-

Parasitic Relationship in Human Contexts:

In human interactions, parasitic behavior typically arises when one individual deftly exploits another's emotions, efforts, or goodwill while providing little to no genuine reciprocity. This relationship involves people who continuously benefit from others' kindness, taking advantage of their resources, such as time, energy, or financial aid, without making any substantial contributions to the relationship. These actions echo the principles of brood parasitism, where one party flourishes at the expense of another, highlighting the complex interplay of dependence and exploitation.

This imbalance can lead to emotional exhaustion for the exploited party, who may begin to feel devalued and manipulated. In contrast, the parasitic individual often remains unaware of the harm they inflict, continuing a cycle of detrimental dynamics. Recognizing these patterns is crucial for fostering healthier, mutually beneficial relationships where both parties actively contribute to and support each other's well-being.

Case Study: Emotional Parasitism in Relationships

Imagine a situation in a relationship where one partner constantly seeks emotional support, financial help, and validation. This can create a notable imbalance. The partner often turns to the other for reassurance during tough moments, requests money for personal needs or projects, and desires recognition for their successes and emotions. Yet, this dependence is seldom reciprocated with an equal amount of care, empathy, or effort from the other partner.

As time goes on, the partner who continually gives starts to feel the weight of this unbalanced relationship. Their emotional reserves become exhausted as they consistently provide support without receiving any in return. Additionally, they may feel financially strained by the constant demands placed upon them, leading to stress and potential instability in their own resources.

This continuous cycle of unreciprocated support can foster feelings of burnout, causing the giving partner to feel unappreciated and taken for granted. As resentment builds, the emotional disconnect between the partners deepens, creating a rift that can weaken the foundation of the relationship. Ultimately, the toll of this imbalance can have profound effects, resulting in long-term dissatisfaction and questioning the viability of their partnership.

✅ Parasitic Relationship Dynamics:

- **Emotional Manipulation:** One partner exploits the other's empathy and commitment.
- **Resource Drain:** The giving partner experiences fatigue, stress, and emotional depletion.
- **Relational Breakdown:** Prolonged parasitism results in trust and emotional connection collapse.

1.4.4 Consequences of Parasitism: The Price of Imbalance

Parasitic relationships, observed both in the natural world and human interactions, can have profound and far-reaching consequences that extend beyond the immediate extraction of resources. In nature, parasites can weaken their hosts over time, compromising their overall health and ability to thrive. This affects the host's chances of survival and disrupts the broader ecosystem, as health-depleted hosts may experience reduced reproductive success and lower resilience to environmental stressors.

In human interactions, parasitism can appear in various forms, such as toxic relationships or exploitative social interactions. Over time, individuals who engage in parasitic behaviors may drain their counterparts' emotional, financial, or social resources, leading to resentment, burnout, and a breakdown of trust. The long-term effects on the host, whether a person or a community, can result in a diminished sense of agency, increased vulnerability to further exploitation, and an erosion of social ties. Thus, both in nature and human society, the consequences of parasitism extend far beyond immediate impacts, ultimately influencing the stability and health of entire systems:

- **Emotional Exhaustion:** Persistent emotional parasitism drains the victim's mental and spiritual well-being.
- **Loss of Trust and Security:** Parasitic relationships erode trust, making it difficult for the host to rebuild meaningful connections.

- **Collapse and Termination:** Left unchecked, parasitism ultimately leads to the breakdown of relationships, organizations, or ecosystems.

Conclusion: Recognizing and Eliminating Parasitic Relationships

Recognizing and addressing parasitic relationships is crucial for fostering vibrant and sustainable connections, whether in personal, organizational, or community contexts. Leaders, families, and community members must actively cultivate awareness to identify patterns of exploitation and manipulation that can drain resources and undermine stability. These parasitic behaviors often manifest as a lack of reciprocity, where one party consistently benefits at the expense of another.

To counteract these harmful traits, fostering relationships based on trust, accountability, and mutual benefit is essential. This requires promoting open communication, establishing clear expectations, and cultivating a respectful culture where everyone feels valued and listened to. By establishing this kind of environment, we create a framework that fosters ecosystems where collaboration and support increases, ultimately leading to greater growth and stability for everyone involved. Ultimately, pursuing reciprocal relationships enables individuals and groups to flourish, ensuring that resources are utilized wisely and efficiently for the common good.

As we move into 1.5 Symbiosis in the Universe, we will explore how cosmic interactions reflect these same principles, offering further insights into the universe's design for interconnectedness and balance.

1.5 Symbiosis in the Universe

Symbiosis is a concept often seen in the natural world, yet its principles resonate far beyond terrestrial ecosystems. The universe operates on fundamental ideas of balance, interdependence, and harmony, creating a complex web of interactions that sustain various forms of existence. For example, the gravitational forces that bind galaxies in intricate dances illustrate how celestial bodies depend on one another to maintain structural integrity across vast cosmic distances.

The life cycle of stars is a fascinating process that includes their formation, nuclear fuel consumption, and their eventual explosive endings. When stars undergo supernova explosions, they release crucial elements into the universe, enriching the interstellar medium. This enrichment sets the stage for creating new stars and planets, showcasing the remarkable interconnectedness of cosmic events.

Although immense and often beyond human comprehension, these grand cosmic phenomena impart significant lessons that are applicable to our lives on Earth. They remind us that the relationships we cultivate thrive on interdependence and mutual support, whether in our personal lives, communities, or workplaces. By embracing these principles, we can foster more meaningful connections that reflect the harmonious balance observed in the universe, ultimately leading to healthier and more resilient relationships.

1.5.1 The Sun and Earth: Life-Sustaining Interdependence

One of the most remarkable examples of cosmic symbiosis is the intricate relationship between the Sun and Earth. The Sun, a massive and radiant sphere of hydrogen and helium, is the primary energy source for our planet. It emits a tremendous amount of light and heat through a process known as nuclear fusion, which occurs in its core. This energy is essential for sustaining life on Earth as it drives the planet's climate systems, fuels photosynthesis in plants, and influences weather patterns. Without the Sun's life-giving energy, Earth's climate would become inhospitable, and the diverse ecosystems that thrive today would not exist.

Earth's unique position in the solar system plays a crucial role in maintaining the delicate balance required for life to flourish. Positioned at the optimal distance from the Sun, Earth resides in the "Goldilocks Zone," where temperatures are neither too hot nor too cold. This ideal location allows for the presence of liquid water, a fundamental prerequisite for life as we know it. Additionally, Earth's axial tilt and rotation create seasons, contributing to the planet's diversity of habitats and biological rhythms. The gravitational forces at play also stabilize Earth's orbit, ensuring consistency in the environmental conditions necessary for sustaining various forms of life. This reciprocal relationship exemplifies the relationship of celestial bodies and highlights how the Sun and Earth, through their unique characteristics, cooperate to support a vibrant and complex biosphere.

☑ Symbiotic Dynamics:

- **Energy Transfer:** The Sun supplies radiant energy that fuels photosynthesis, sustains ecosystems, and regulates Earth's climate.
- **Orbital Stability:** Earth's gravitational relationship with the Sun maintains a stable orbit, preventing it from drifting into the cold abyss of space.
- **Climate Regulation:** The Earth's atmosphere protects life by filtering harmful solar radiation and maintaining a habitable temperature.

How This Relates to Human Relationships:

Just as the Sun and Earth maintain a delicate balance that supports life, successful human relationships depend on a similar equilibrium of giving and receiving. Leaders who consistently invest time, energy, and resources in their teams foster a nurturing environment where individuals can truly thrive. This investment goes beyond mere oversight; it encompasses offering guidance, providing mentorship, and sharing invaluable resources that empower team members to reach their full potential.

When leaders take the time to connect personally and actively support their teams, they foster a culture of trust and psychological safety. In response, team members often reciprocate with loyalty, unwavering dedication, and innovative ideas that propel the organization forward. This dynamic interaction cultivates a powerful cycle of mutual growth, benefiting both the individual and the organization, ultimately leading to a stronger, more resilient team that can adapt and excel in an ever-changing landscape.

Case Study: Mentorship in Leadership

The relationship between Oprah Winfrey and Maya Angelou illustrates a deep, symbiotic connection, similar to that of the Sun and Earth. Maya Angelou, renowned for her literary talent and profound insights, served as a mentor to Oprah Winfrey during pivotal moments in Winfrey's life and career. Through her guidance, Angelou provided invaluable wisdom, encouragement, and emotional support that shaped Winfrey's identity and professional trajectory. In this nurturing relationship, Angelou's teachings inspired Winfrey to embrace her own voice as a storyteller and advocate for social change.

Oprah Winfrey's extraordinary achievements and wide-reaching influence revitalized interest in Angelou's literary works and life philosophies. Through her platform, Winfrey introduced Angelou's writings to a broad audience, ensuring that her legacy resonated with new generations. By honoring Angelou's insights through interviews, book clubs, and public endorsements, Winfrey not only paid tribute to her mentor but also reinforced Angelou's significance in modern culture. Their relationship thus illustrates a powerful cycle of inspiration and legacy creation, with each woman elevating the other in significant and transformative ways.

✅ Relational Symbiosis Dynamics:

- **Mutual Growth:** Angelou's mentorship empowered Winfrey to become an influential media mogul.
- **Amplified Legacy:** Winfrey's platform brought renewed recognition to Angelou's contributions.
- **Sustained Influence:** Their relationship demonstrated how mutual investment creates a long-term impact.

1.5.2 The Moon and Earth: Gravitational Harmony and Stability

The Moon, Earth's only natural satellite, is essential not only for maintaining the planet's stability but also for sustaining life itself. Its gravitational pull initiates and regulates the tides, creating intricate and rhythmic cycles that significantly influence marine ecosystems and coastal environments. These tidal movements play a vital role in nutrient distribution, sediment transport, and the spawning cycles of various marine species, enhancing biodiversity in oceanic habitats.

Moreover, the Moon's gravitational influence stabilizes Earth's axial tilt, which is essential for maintaining a consistent angle as the planet orbits the Sun. This stability regulates seasonal variations and climate patterns, ensuring the conditions necessary for life can thrive. Without the Moon's moderating effect, Earth would likely experience drastic fluctuations in its rotation, resulting in erratic weather patterns, extreme temperature changes, and prolonged periods of drought or excessive rainfall. Such instability could create an environment where many existing species face immense challenges, threatening biodiversity and ecosystem resilience.

Essentially, the Moon is a crucial component in maintaining the balance of Earth's systems. It influences ocean currents, weather patterns, and atmospheric conditions. By promoting a stable climate and supporting numerous ecological processes, the Moon plays a vital role in creating and sustaining a hospitable environment for diverse life forms. Its significance extends beyond aesthetics, establishing it as a key ally in life's ongoing journey on our planet.

Symbiotic Dynamics:

- **Tidal Influence:** The Moon's gravitational force creates ocean tides that regulate marine ecosystems.
- **Axial Stability:** The Moon stabilizes Earth's axial tilt, preventing extreme climate fluctuations.
- **Rhythmic Cycles:** Lunar cycles influence biological rhythms in various species.

How This Relates to Emotional and Relational Stability:

Just as the Moon plays a crucial role in stabilizing the Earth's tilt and rotation, emotional support, accountability, and consistency are vital for fostering stability within relationships. When individuals consistently provide a steady presence and emotional grounding, they create a nurturing environment where trust can grow, security can be established, and resilience can flourish. Emotional support involves actively listening to and validating each other's feelings, fostering a sense of belonging and understanding. Accountability means taking responsibility for one's actions and words, establishing a foundation of trust that partners can depend on. Consistency is pivotal in reinforcing this foundation, ensuring that individuals can rely on one another during both challenging and joyful times. Together, these elements weave a rich tapestry of connection, enabling relationships to endure life's inevitable ups and downs.

Case Study: Emotional Stability in Marriages

The marriage of former U.S. President Barack Obama and Michelle Obama exemplifies the profound stabilizing influence that emotional support can have in a partnership.

During President Barack Obama's tenure, Michelle's unwavering support and nurturing presence provided him with a crucial foundation to navigate the immense pressures and challenges of leadership. Her ability to maintain balance and groundedness enabled Barack to focus on his responsibilities while knowing he had a dependable source of encouragement.

On the other hand, President Barack Obama's profound respect for Michelle and acknowledgment of her talents encouraged her to rise as a powerful leader and advocate. Together, they created a partnership in which their mutual support not only strengthened their personal connection but also boosted their individual influence in society. Their relationship exemplifies how love, respect, and emotional stability nurture resilience and motivate both personal and professional development, ultimately defining their legacy as a dynamic duo dedicated to progress and positive change.

Relational Stability Dynamics:

- **Mutual Support:** Both partners contributed emotional stability during challenging times.
- **Shared Accountability:** They held one another accountable for their personal and professional growth.
- **Resilience in Adversity:** Their emotional connection provided stability amid political and personal challenges.

1.5.3 Stellar Life Cycle: Birth, Death, and Regeneration

The life cycle of stars symbolizes transformation, renewal, and the enduring legacy of existence. It begins within massive nebulae, vast swirling clouds of gas and dust rich in hydrogen and helium. Eventually, these clouds undergo gravitational collapse, leading to the formation of protostars. As a protostar gathers more material, its core temperature rises, ultimately initiating nuclear fusion and marking the birth of a new star. Throughout their lives, stars undergo the remarkable process of nuclear fusion, converting hydrogen into helium and releasing an immense amount of energy in the form of light and heat. This process not only sustains the star but also enriches the surrounding cosmos by creating heavier elements such as carbon, oxygen, and iron, which are essential for the formation of planets and the emergence of life.

As stars age and exhaust their nuclear fuel, their fates diverge. Smaller stars, like our Sun, will gradually expand into red giants before shedding their outer layers, leaving behind a dense core known as a white dwarf. In contrast, massive stars end their lives in cataclysmic explosions called supernovae. These dramatic events scatter elements across the universe, seeding new stars and planetary systems, thereby continuing the cycle of creation. Ultimately, the life cycle of stars not only reflects the complex processes of the universe but also underscores the interconnectedness of all matter, illustrating how the remnants of ancient stars contribute to the birth of new worlds and the continuation of life itself.

Symbiotic Dynamics:

- **Element Formation:** Stars produce essential elements like carbon, oxygen, and iron, which are dispersed into the universe upon their death.
- **Cosmic Recycling:** Supernovae enrich the universe with raw materials that give rise to new celestial bodies.

- **Interconnected Legacy:** Each generation of stars contributes to the formation of future planetary systems.

How This Relates to Leadership and Legacy:

Just as stars in the universe undergo nuclear fusion to create new elements essential for sustaining future life, effective leaders cultivate environments that empower, equip, and inspire their successors to carry forward the organization's mission. Through thoughtful succession planning, leaders invest not only in the immediate needs of their teams but also in the enduring health and vitality of the organization itself. By mentoring and developing emerging leaders, they ensure that their vision and values are deeply ingrained in the culture, allowing their influence to persist long after their tenure has ended. This proactive approach not only enhances the organization's resilience but also leaves a profound and lasting legacy, paving the way for future generations to thrive and innovate in alignment with the established mission.

Case Study: Bill Gates and Microsoft's Leadership Transition

Bill Gates, the visionary co-founder of Microsoft, exemplified stellar symbiosis in his approach to leadership by facilitating a smooth transition to Satya Nadella as CEO. Recognizing the importance of cultivating future leaders, Gates took an active role in mentoring Nadella and shared insights from his extensive experience at the helm of the company. This intentional investment in leadership development not only prepared Nadella for the challenges ahead but also laid a strong foundation for a transformative era at Microsoft.

Under Nadella's guidance, Microsoft experienced a significant cultural shift, marked by a focus on empathy, innovation, and resilience. He cultivated an environment that promoted collaboration and inclusivity, enabling diverse ideas to thrive. This cultural transformation not only respected Gates' legacy of innovation but also redefined Microsoft's identity, positioning the company to succeed in the fast-changing tech landscape. Nadella's leadership strategy successfully connected the company's rich past with its promising future, showcasing the impact of thoughtful transition and visionary leadership.

✅ **Leadership Legacy Dynamics:**

- **Succession Planning:** Gates prepared Nadella to lead effectively.

- **Cultural Transformation:** Nadella built on Gates' foundation while introducing new values.

- **Sustained Innovation:** Microsoft's continued growth reflects the success of their Symbiotic Leadership™ transition.

1.5.4 Planetary Orbits and Gravitational Balance: Order in Chaos

Planetary systems are intricately held together by the fundamental forces of gravity, functioning within a delicate balance that not only prevents chaos but also sustains a profound cosmic order. Each planet's orbit is shaped by the gravitational pull exerted by larger celestial bodies, such as stars and other planets, contributing to the overall stability and harmony of the solar system. This dynamic interplay of gravitational forces creates a symphony of motion, where the path of each celestial body is both predictable and essential for maintaining order in the system.

The mutual gravitational interactions among these celestial bodies help minimize the risk of catastrophic collisions, creating a stable environment where planets can thrive. This gravitational ballet is crucial, as even slight alterations in a planet's orbit could lead to significant consequences, affecting not only that planet but potentially the entire solar system. Thus, the intricate relationships among gravitational forces not only govern the movement of planets but also uphold the very fabric of cosmic tranquility.

Symbiotic Dynamics:

- **Orbital Stability:** Planets maintain equilibrium, preventing catastrophic disruptions.
- **Predictable Motion:** Gravitational balance sustains consistent cosmic rhythms.
- **Interconnected Security:** The gravitational pull of larger planets shields smaller planets from potential impacts.

How This Relates to Organizational Balance:

Just as planetary orbits are essential for maintaining cosmic stability, organizations thrive when their leaders effectively balance authority, accountability, and autonomy within their teams. This delicate equilibrium ensures that individuals in departments and teams operate not just independently but also collaboratively, guided by a shared sense of purpose and mutual accountability. When each member understands their roles and responsibilities and feels empowered to take initiative, organizations can cultivate a culture of innovation and creativity.

Furthermore, this collaborative framework promotes transparent communication and trust, which are essential for overcoming challenges and capitalizing on opportunities. As departments synchronize their objectives with the organization's overarching goals, they foster a unified strategy that strengthens both stability and adaptability. In the end, this deliberate approach results in sustainable success, marked by ongoing improvement and resilience in a constantly changing business environment.

Case Study: Google's Organizational Structure

Google's approach to maintaining organizational balance exemplifies the principles of symbiosis in a corporate environment. The company utilizes a matrix organizational structure that not only encourages collaboration among various departments but also ensures that accountability is preserved at every level. This structure enables teams to effectively share ideas and resources, fostering an innovative atmosphere while allowing individuals within those teams to maintain creative autonomy.

Moreover, Google's intentional balance between innovation, accountability, and structure is a crucial factor contributing to its sustained success as a global technology leader. By achieving this balance, Google can swiftly adapt to market changes, embrace new technologies, and continuously improve its products and services. This distinctive model fosters a dynamic workplace culture where employees feel empowered to take risks and pursue innovative projects, ultimately driving the company's growth and reinforcing its competitive advantage in the technology sector.

✅ Organizational Symbiosis Dynamics:

- **Aligned Autonomy:** Departments operate with freedom while aligning with organizational goals.
- **Mutual Accountability:** Collaboration and communication maintain balance.
- **Sustained Success:** The organization succeeds due to a culture of innovation and trust.

1.5.5 Black Holes and Event Horizons: The Consequences of Imbalance

The universe thrives on the principles of balance and mutual benefit, yet black holes starkly illustrate the dire consequences of imbalance. Formed from the catastrophic collapse of massive stars at the end of their life cycles, black holes possess gravitational forces so immense that nothing, not even light, can escape their event horizons, making them some of the most enigmatic entities in the cosmos. These cosmic phenomena serve as powerful symbols of the destructive nature inherent in unchecked power and unsustainable consumption.

When a star exhausts its nuclear fuel, it can no longer sustain the outward pressure needed to balance the inward pull of gravity, resulting in its implosion. The resulting black hole draws in surrounding matter, often disrupting nearby stellar systems and consuming gas and dust at an alarming rate. This process not only emphasizes the sheer power of such celestial objects but also serves as a warning about the consequences of overexploitation and a lack of equilibrium in any system, whether in nature or human societies. The existence of black holes prompts profound reflection on the importance of maintaining balance in our own interactions and the need for responsible stewardship of resources.

✅ Imbalance Dynamics:

- **Resource Consumption:** Black holes consume surrounding matter, destabilizing neighboring systems.
- **Collapse and Isolation:** The event horizon traps all nearby matter, preventing escape.
- **Loss of Symbiotic Potential:** Black holes disrupt the equilibrium of nearby celestial bodies.

How This Relates to Toxic Leadership and Relationships:

Similar to black holes in space, toxic leaders and unhealthy relationships can severely impact their surroundings by draining valuable resources, energy, and trust. Those caught in their gravitational pull often feel drained, demoralized, and disillusioned. When ambition, power, or the desire for control spiral out of control, they create a toxic environment that leads to significant emotional and psychological harm.

This unchecked influence can cause organizations and interpersonal relationships to deteriorate, ultimately collapsing under the immense weight of imbalance and negativity. Such behaviors undermine productivity and morale while also instigating a ripple effect that affects the broader community, eroding trust and cooperation among individuals. It is crucial to recognize and address these destructive patterns before they lead to irreversible damage.

Case Study: Toxic Leadership in Uber's Early Culture

The early leadership at Uber was characterized by a relentless pursuit of market dominance, frequently prioritizing aggressive competition over ethical considerations. This approach nurtured a culture steeped in fear, where employees felt pressured to meet unrealistic targets, often at the expense of their well-being. The company's rapid expansion during this period, while impressive, was tarnished by instances of exploitation and a lack of accountability, both internally among staff and externally in its dealings with regulators and competitors.

Reports of unethical practices within Uber, including aggressive tactics against drivers and competitors, began to emerge. This situation, combined with a dismissive attitude toward regulatory scrutiny, created a significant shift in the company's atmosphere. Furthermore, concerns about harassment and workplace inequality intensified internal discontent among employees.

Ultimately, the repercussions of this toxic culture became clear, resulting in significant leadership changes and a damaged public image. The fallout compelled the company to confront its practices and implement reforms aimed at rebuilding trust and fostering a more equitable workplace. While Uber continues to strive for success, the lessons learned from its early tumultuous years remain crucial for its ongoing evolution.

Toxic Leadership Dynamics:

- **Unchecked Power:** Leaders prioritized growth over ethics and well-being.

- **Cultural Collapse:** Employee morale and trust deteriorated.
- **Restorative Intervention:** Leadership changes were necessary to restore balance and trust.

Conclusion: Cosmic Lessons for Thriving Relationships

The universe's intricate systems of balance, interdependence, and regeneration provide profound insights into the foundations of symbiotic relationships. The Sun, with its sustaining energy, fuels life on Earth by enabling photosynthesis and supporting the food chain that sustains countless species. Meanwhile, the Moon plays a crucial role in regulating tides, which in turn influence marine ecosystems and the creatures that inhabit them. Beyond these celestial bodies, the life cycles of stars, whose birth, evolution, and eventual death contribute to the formation of new elements, remind us of the interconnectedness of all things.

These cosmic events symbolize human interactions, demonstrating that mutual investment, trust, and accountability are essential for healthy relationships. Much like ecosystems thrive when every component fulfills its role, our communities can prosper when individuals actively support each other, fostering an atmosphere abundant in growth, stability, and resilience. By embracing these universal principles, we can forge deeper connections and achieve a harmonious existence that reflects the natural world's intrinsic wisdom.

As we move into 1.6 The Role of Reciprocity, we will explore how the principle of reciprocal exchange ensures the longevity of relationships, organizations, and ecosystems.

1.6 The Role of Reciprocity: Cultivating Mutual Benefit in Relationships

Reciprocity is vital to symbiosis, acting as a key force that sustains mutually beneficial relationships across various contexts. In nature, reciprocity manifests in numerous forms as organisms exchange resources, services, and support, fostering conditions where both parties thrive. A prominent example is the relationship between pollinators and flowering plants, in which bees gather nectar while assisting the plants' reproduction through pollination. This mutual dependence not only increases the survival chances of individual species but also improves the overall health of ecosystems.

In human relationships, whether personal, professional, or spiritual, reciprocity creates a balanced exchange that encourages both parties to invest in and benefit from the connection. In personal relationships, this could mean friends supporting each other emotionally or during times of need, while in professional settings, colleagues might share knowledge and resources to achieve common goals. Such exchanges build trust, deepen connections, and foster a sense of community.

On the other hand, when reciprocity is lacking, relationships can become one-sided, leading to feelings of exploitation and resentment. This imbalance can undermine trust and deplete resources, jeopardizing the sustainability of the relationship. In serious cases, it may even result in a breakdown, as one party could withdraw or disengage, unable to tolerate an unhealthy dynamic. Therefore, fostering reciprocity is vital not only for the well-being of relationships but also for the durability of the connections we establish in all aspects of life.

1.6.1 Understanding Reciprocity: The Foundation of Mutual Exchange

Reciprocity is the act of responding positively to positive actions, promoting a mutually rewarding relationship between individuals or organizations. This principle establishes a beneficial cycle where each party enjoys the fruits of their contributions and is motivated to persist in supportive behaviors. Fundamentally, reciprocity fosters trust and collaboration, inspiring participants to engage in relationships defined by fairness, integrity, and mutual respect.

This interaction is essential in various situations, including personal relationships, professional environments, and broader societal interactions. By fostering a culture of reciprocity, individuals and organizations can cultivate a sense of community and collaboration, which promotes innovation, loyalty, and sustainable growth. Embracing reciprocity essentially involves not just obtaining immediate rewards; it requires a long-term commitment to partnership and shared success.

Types of Reciprocity:

1. **Direct Reciprocity:** A direct exchange where one party reciprocates a favor or service to the other.
    - *Example:* A mentor who invests time and knowledge into developing a mentee receives loyalty, dedication, and gratitude in return.
2. **Indirect Reciprocity:** A system in which positive actions create a ripple effect, encouraging others to reciprocate through third parties.

- *Example:* A leader who fosters an atmosphere of generosity and support motivates employees to share these values with their colleagues and communities.
3. **Generalized Reciprocity:** A continual commitment to contribute without expecting immediate returns, trusting that positive actions will eventually yield benefits in unexpected ways.
    - *Example:* A nonprofit organization that assists underserved communities without seeking immediate gain often garners long-term support from donors and volunteers.

Leadership Insight:

In leadership, the principle of reciprocity plays a crucial role in cultivating a workplace culture where employees genuinely feel valued and inspired to put forth their best efforts. When leaders actively invest in their teams through initiatives like mentorship programs, regular recognition of achievements, and opportunities for empowerment, they create an environment that encourages personal and professional growth. This kind of commitment not only boosts morale but also fosters a sense of belonging among team members.

As a result, Leaders who prioritize these reciprocal relationships often experience heightened loyalty from their employees, which can translate into increased productivity and a surge of innovative ideas. In a workplace where employees feel their contributions are appreciated, creativity thrives, collaboration is encouraged, and problem-solving becomes a collective endeavor. Ultimately, investing in positive leader-employee dynamics generates a cycle of mutual respect and benefit, significantly enhancing overall organizational performance.

1.6.2 Reciprocity in Business: Building Trust and Loyalty

Reciprocity is essential in the corporate sector for establishing trust and promoting effective collaboration, both of which are critical for sustainable growth. Organizations that nurture reciprocal relationships with employees, customers, and partners develop vibrant ecosystems that fuel loyalty, innovation, and resilience. By emphasizing transparent communication and mutual respect, these companies cultivate a culture where everyone feels appreciated and engaged. This reciprocal relationship boosts employee morale and retention while fostering a stronger connection between customers and the brand, resulting in heightened customer loyalty and advocacy.

Moreover, collaborations based on reciprocity can ignite innovative partnerships, as all parties involved are keen to share insights and resources for mutual benefits. This approach not only enhances problem-solving skills but also fosters a culture of continuous improvement and adaptability. By embracing reciprocal principles, organizations can create a nurturing environment that strengthens relationships, encouraging both individual and collective success, while ensuring long-term sustainability in an ever-evolving marketplace.

Case Study: Costco's Commitment to Employees and Customers

Costco Wholesale exemplifies how the principle of reciprocity can lead to business success. By prioritizing fair wages and comprehensive benefits for its employees, Costco fosters a workplace built on mutual respect and appreciation. This strategy is especially significant in the highly competitive retail sector, where many businesses often sacrifice employee compensation to cut costs.

Costco's dedication to workforce investment yields real advantages. By providing competitive salaries, health insurance, retirement plans, and generous paid time off, the company boosts employee satisfaction and reduces turnover rates. This stability fosters a more experienced and knowledgeable workforce, leading to increased productivity levels.

Furthermore, Costco's positive workplace culture inspires employees to excel in providing exceptional customer service. When employees feel valued, they tend to show increased loyalty and commitment to the company, thereby reinforcing their dedication to Costco's core values. This, in turn, creates a beneficial cycle: satisfied employees lead to happy customers, which ultimately enhances the company's profitability and bolsters its reputation in the retail industry.

Reciprocal Dynamics:

- **Employee Investment:** Costco's focus on fair wages and benefits fosters a motivated and engaged workforce.
- **Customer Loyalty:** Outstanding customer service advances repeat business and brand loyalty.
- **Sustainable Growth:** The reciprocity between the company, employees, and customers guarantees long-term success.

Leadership Lesson:

Leaders who promote a culture of reciprocity are vital in creating an environment where team members feel valued and supported. By investing in their teams through professional development, recognizing achievements, and maintaining open communication, they enhance employee engagement significantly. This increased sense of belonging and purpose not only lifts morale but also fosters greater productivity and innovation. Furthermore, when employees feel valued and are encouraged to return that support, it naturally leads to higher customer satisfaction.

Effective teamwork and mutual trust enhance the understanding of and response to customer needs, ultimately fostering loyalty and stronger relationships. This culture of shared success and growth drives organizational advancement. Trust, developed through reciprocity, strengthens a collective commitment to shared goals, creating a solid foundation for sustained success. Essentially, highlighting reciprocity within an organization fosters a dynamic environment where both employees and customers engage more profoundly with the organization's mission and vision.

1.6.3 Reciprocity in Personal Relationships: Strengthening Emotional Bonds

Reciprocity is vital in personal relationships, enhancing emotional security, trust, and closeness. When people invest their time, energy, and sincere care into their connections, they create an atmosphere filled with mutual support and encouragement. This back-and-forth of giving not only deepens the connection between partners but also promotes personal growth for both individuals.

By ensuring that both individuals meaningfully contribute to the relationship, reciprocity helps create a healthy balance that reduces the risk of one-sided interactions. Such an imbalance can lead to emotional exhaustion, resentment, and a decline in trust, making it essential for both partners to participate in a cycle of giving and receiving. Ultimately, this mutual commitment to nurturing the relationship not only strengthens emotional connections but also fosters resilience, allowing both partners to face life's challenges together with greater strength and understanding.

Relationship Insight:

In every type of relationship, whether it's a marriage, friendship, or family bond, the principle of reciprocity plays a crucial role in fostering emotional stability and encouraging personal growth. When both individuals actively participate in the relationship through acts of kindness, empathy, and encouragement, they create a strong foundation of trust and resilience. This shared investment not only deepens their connection but also fosters a warm environment where everyone feels valued and understood. As they face challenges together and celebrate each other's victories, the bond grows stronger, leading to a deeper understanding and emotional closeness over time. Ultimately, it's this beautiful balance of giving and receiving that keeps healthy relationships thriving and brings lasting joy to all involved.

1.6.4 Reciprocity in Leadership: Empowering Teams and Organizations

Reciprocal leadership is a flexible and transformative approach that emphasizes creating a mutually beneficial relationship between leaders and their teams. This model transcends traditional leadership styles by prioritizing continuous give-and-take interactions in which leaders actively invest time, resources, and support in the personal and professional development of their team members. Such investments not only foster an environment conducive to individual growth and innovation but also encourage meaningful contributions to the organization's overall success.

In this reciprocal engagement, team members will likely respond with increased loyalty, dedication, and strong commitment to the organization's mission. The relationship creates a powerful feedback loop: motivated employees feel empowered to take initiative, propose innovative ideas, and contribute to problem-solving, knowing their leaders genuinely value their input and are committed to their success. Leaders who prioritize this reciprocity play a crucial role in cultivating a culture defined by trust, accountability, and mutual respect within their teams. They establish open lines of communication that encourage transparency and dialogue, promote collaboration by leveraging each team member's diverse perspectives and skills, and regularly recognize and celebrate individuals' unique contributions.

A supportive and inclusive environment enhances team morale and strengthens performance and organizational resilience. When team members feel valued and recognized for their contributions, they are more likely to excel in their roles, leading to increased productivity and innovation. This commitment to mutual leadership fosters a vibrant organizational culture where leaders and team members can flourish together.

Case Study: Satya Nadella's Leadership at Microsoft

When Satya Nadella took the helm of Microsoft in 2014, he embarked on a transformative journey to shift the company's culture toward one that prioritizes empathy, collaboration, and empowerment among its employees. Recognizing the need for adaptability in a rapidly changing tech landscape, Nadella introduced a growth mindset philosophy, encouraging employees to embrace challenges, learn from failures, and continuously develop their skills. This approach fostered a more inclusive and innovative environment and significantly boosted employee engagement and morale.

Under Nadella's leadership, Microsoft invested significantly in employee development programs, enhancing training opportunities and fostering a culture of lifelong learning. This dedication to growth and collaboration has resulted in a remarkable resurgence of the company's innovative capabilities, demonstrated by the successful launch of new products and services resonating well in the market. Ultimately, Nadella's cultural overhaul has revitalized Microsoft's internal dynamics and positioned the company for significant market success, illustrating how effective leadership can transform an organization from within.

☑ Reciprocal Leadership Dynamics:

- **Empowerment and Trust:** Nadella empowered employees by fostering a culture of learning and collaboration.
- **Increased Innovation:** Employees reciprocated by driving technological advancements and embracing change.

- **Sustainable Growth:** Microsoft's resurgence reflected the strength of a reciprocal leadership model.

Leadership Insight:

Reciprocal leadership transforms our perception of leaders, viewing them not merely as authority figures but as dedicated guardians focused on the growth and well-being of their teams. This approach underscores the importance of building relationships and creating an environment where team members feel valued and supported. By emphasizing the personal and professional development of others, leaders cultivate a culture that enhances loyalty, sparks creativity, and promotes accountability among team members. Such an environment not only elevates individual performance but also strengthens collaboration and innovation, paving the way for collective success. By nurturing the strengths and aspirations of their teams, leaders empower individuals to take ownership of their roles and make significant contributions to the organization's objectives.

1.6.5 The Consequences of a Lack of Reciprocity

In personal, professional, or organizational relationships, a lack of reciprocity creates a significant imbalance that can lead to several negative consequences. When there is no mutual exchange, one party may feel exploited, contributing more than they receive. This imbalance can foster resentment, especially among those who feel that their contributions or sacrifices are overlooked or devalued.

Consequently, trust, a fundamental cornerstone of any healthy relationship, begins to diminish. Trust takes time to build, but can be quickly dismantled when one party feels that their efforts are not recognized or appreciated. In such environments, communication often deteriorates; individuals become hesitant to express their thoughts or concerns, fearing that their input will continue to be disregarded.

Additionally, the emotional impact can be profound. Individuals in one-sided relationships often feel neglected and isolated, which may result in disengagement and lower morale. This can translate to reduced productivity and increased turnover in workplace scenarios as employees seek more equitable and supportive environments. Ultimately, the absence of reciprocity can irreparably harm relationships, leading to a breakdown of connection and collaboration.

Consequences of Absent Reciprocity:

- **Emotional Exhaustion:** One-sided relationships result in burnout and emotional exhaustion.
- **Erosion of Trust:** When reciprocity is missing, trust erodes, complicating rebuilding efforts.
- **Relational Breakdown:** Relationships weaken and eventually fall apart without mutual investment.

Leadership Insight:

Organizations prioritizing profits over their employees' well-being often foster a toxic culture lacking reciprocity and mutual respect. In such environments, employees may feel exploited or unappreciated, resulting in emotional detachment from their work and the organization. This disengagement leads to several negative consequences, including high turnover rates, as talented individuals seek more supportive workplaces. Additionally, a decline in morale reduces employee enthusiasm and inhibits collaboration and creativity, ultimately causing decreased productivity and an overall decline in organizational performance. Overlooking these issues can initiate a vicious cycle that jeopardizes both employee satisfaction and business success.

1.6.6 Cultivating a Culture of Reciprocity: Practical Steps

Creating environments where reciprocity thrives requires intentionality, empathy, and a strong commitment to mutual benefit. In personal relationships, this involves actively listening to and valuing each other's perspectives, ensuring that both parties feel acknowledged and appreciated. In leadership contexts, fostering reciprocity promotes an inclusive culture where team members are encouraged to share their thoughts and contributions, ultimately leading to increased engagement and collaboration. Similarly, in organizational settings, nurturing a sense of reciprocity ensures that everyone feels their input is vital, which boosts morale and drives innovation and productivity. By prioritizing these principles, we can create spaces where all individuals feel valued, heard, and empowered, paving the way for stronger connections and a more harmonious environment.

Practical Strategies for Cultivating Reciprocity:

1. **Practice Active Listening:** Show genuine interest in understanding others' perspectives and needs. Ask open-ended questions and provide feedback to demonstrate engagement.
2. **Acknowledge Contributions:** Recognize and celebrate the efforts and successes of others. This can be through verbal praise, written notes, or public acknowledgment in group settings.

3. **Offer Support Without Expectation:** Demonstrate generosity and service, trusting that positive actions will create a ripple effect. Volunteer your time or resources to aid others without anticipating anything in return.
4. **Set Clear Expectations:** Establish boundaries and ensure that all parties understand their roles and responsibilities. Clarify what you hope to achieve collectively and outline how each person can contribute.
5. **Model Reciprocity:** Lead by example, demonstrating fairness, empathy, and a commitment to mutual growth. When others see you acting with integrity and kindness, they are more likely to follow suit.
6. **Create Opportunities for Collaboration:** Encourage teamwork by setting up joint projects or group activities where everyone can contribute and benefit from each other's skills.
7. **Share Knowledge and Resources:** Be open with your expertise and resources. Whether it's sharing information, tools, or connections, this fosters a culture of help and reciprocity.
8. **Encourage Open Communication:** Create an environment where individuals feel safe to express their thoughts and concerns. Transparent communication strengthens trust and mutual respect.
9. **Solicit Feedback:** Regularly ask for input on your actions and decisions. This shows that you value others' opinions and helps create a space for reciprocal dialogue.
10. **Be Mindful of Non-Verbal Cues:** Pay attention to body language and emotions, both yours and

those of others. Non-verbal communication can significantly impact relationships and the perception of reciprocity.
11. **Cultivate Patience:** Understand that reciprocity may not happen immediately. Be patient and allow relationships to build naturally over time.
12. **Celebrate Collective Wins:** Regularly take time to acknowledge and celebrate milestones or achievements as a group. This reinforces the bond and highlights the interdependence of efforts.
13. **Maintain Flexibility:** Be adaptable in your approaches and willing to compromise. This openness encourages others to reciprocate your flexibility and support.
14. **Follow Up:** After providing support or assistance, check in with others to see how they are doing. This gesture reinforces your care and commitment to mutual well-being.
15. **Encourage a Culture of Gratitude:** Foster an environment where expressing gratitude is commonplace. When people feel appreciated, they are more likely to continue engaging in reciprocal interactions.

By adopting these strategies, you can cultivate a profound sense of reciprocity in your relationships, encouraging collaboration and mutual development. This method not only reinforces bonds but also fosters a supportive environment where everyone can prosper together.

Conclusion: Reciprocity as the Lifeblood of Thriving Relationships

Reciprocity serves as a vital foundation that nurtures and sustains flourishing relationships in all areas of life, whether personal, professional, or spiritual. This principle of mutual exchange creates a vibrant atmosphere where trust, accountability, and mutual respect can flourish. When individuals and organizations consciously embrace reciprocity, they cultivate environments that encourage steadfast loyalty while igniting innovation and facilitating meaningful growth.

In personal relationships, reciprocity involves actively participating in heartfelt give-and-take interactions that strengthen emotional bonds. This openness creates an environment where communication flows freely, allowing individuals to feel safe in offering and receiving support, thereby fostering a deeper connection. In professional settings, it appears as a spirit of collaborative teamwork, with each member recognizing and valuing the unique contributions of others. This appreciation enhances productivity and creativity, transforming the workplace into a dynamic hub of inspiration and progress.

Reciprocity promotes an enriching sense of interconnectedness and shared purpose. It nurtures a vibrant community where individuals support one another, guided by common values and ambitions. This collective growth enhances one's personal journey, providing a sense of belonging and fulfillment.

By actively prioritizing reciprocal relationships, we establish a solid foundation for lasting partnerships that foster continuous growth and spark meaningful change. These connections are the foundation of a vibrant life, enabling us to face challenges with resilience and celebrate our triumphs together. Through mutual support and understanding, we create an environment where each person can flourish, and our collective journey becomes a rich tapestry woven with shared experiences and aspirations.

As we move into 1.7 Mutual Growth and Accountability, we will explore how these principles further solidify the foundations of symbiotic relationships, driving continuous improvement and shared success. 🌱

1.7 Mutual Growth and Accountability: Sustaining Symbiotic Relationships

Thriving symbiotic relationships are built on the core principles of mutual growth and accountability, forming a foundation for lasting connections. These principles cultivate an environment where both parties can succeed together, creating a culture of continuous development rooted in shared values and aspirations. By investing in mutual growth, individuals actively support each other's goals, talents, and ambitions, recognizing that success isn't a zero-sum game. The accomplishments of one partner enhance the strength and resilience of both, providing a strong base for their partnership to flourish.

Accountability is essential in this setting, cultivating an environment where both partners maintain high standards of integrity and excellence. This involves honest, open communication, giving constructive feedback, and showing a readiness to tackle challenges together. Amid widespread relationship obstacles like complacency, miscommunication, or lack of direction, this steadfast dedication to mutual growth and accountability acts as a safeguard against stagnation and conflict.

These principles not only promote personal advancement but also strengthen the overall resilience of the relationship. A foundation grounded in trust, transparency, and shared responsibility enables both partners to achieve mutual growth and accountability, enhancing their ability to face challenges confidently. This collaboration keeps relationships dynamic, flexible, and prepared for lasting success, with each partner motivating the other to reach new heights. As both individuals dedicate time and energy to nurturing these values, they create a deeper, more fulfilling connection that adapts to their personal and collective experiences.

1.7.1 Understanding Mutual Growth: A Commitment to Shared Development

Mutual growth goes beyond a simple idea; it is a continuous journey nurtured when both parties in a relationship actively contribute to each other's development. This collaboration fosters a supportive environment where learning, adaptability, and progress thrive. More than mere involvement, mutual growth represents a joint expedition where individuals, teams, and organizations work closely together to advance, recognizing that their successes are interconnected.

In this collaborative environment, each participant contributes their unique strengths, diverse experiences, and personal aspirations. When these elements align with shared goals, they create a synergy that enhances individual capabilities while fostering a collective vision that uplifts the entire group. This shared vision is crucial as it clarifies purpose and direction, motivating all members to strive for excellence.

Central to this process are ongoing feedback channels, transparent communication, and a steadfast readiness to adapt as situations evolve. These components foster a culture of creativity and innovation, allowing new ideas and solutions to emerge. When individuals feel secure in sharing their thoughts and suggestions, it enhances their sense of ownership and commitment to the relationship.

Ultimately, mutual growth demonstrates a deep commitment to each other's success. It encourages impactful interactions grounded in trust, respect, and empathy, strengthening relationships and significantly enhancing outcomes, both personally and professionally. As both parties participate in this journey, they achieve their individual goals and contribute to the overall success of their shared efforts.

Core Elements of Mutual Growth:

1. **Continuous Learning:** Engaging in ongoing education and skill enhancement.
2. **Constructive Feedback:** Providing and receiving feedback that fosters improvement.
3. **Goal Alignment:** Ensuring that personal and organizational goals are mutually supportive.
4. **Adaptability and Innovation:** Encouraging exploration and experimentation to adapt to changing circumstances.

Leadership Insight:

Leaders who prioritize shared growth play a crucial role in creating an environment that empowers their teams to take charge of their professional development. By promoting autonomy and accountability, these leaders foster a culture that nurtures curiosity, sparks innovation, and instills a commitment to excellence. When leaders invest in their teams, whether through training, mentorship, or resource allocation, they build a workplace where individuals feel valued, respected, challenged, and motivated to exceed their own expectations. This supportive environment encourages employees to seek new knowledge, embrace creative solutions, and strive for continuous improvement, resulting in enhanced performance and collective success. Thus, the focus on shared growth not only propels individual careers but also advances the overall progress of the organization.

Case Study: Google's Investment in Employee Growth

Google's steadfast commitment to advancing collective growth within its organization illustrates the transformative effects of investing in its people. A notable initiative called the "20% Time" policy permits employees to allocate up to 20% of their workweek to innovative ideas and passion projects that may not directly align with their primary job responsibilities. This flexibility cultivates a culture of continuous learning and creativity, encouraging employees to think outside the box and embrace their entrepreneurial spirit.

By promoting this kind of work environment, Google has effectively nurtured a culture where experimentation and collaboration can flourish. This strategy has resulted in pioneering products that have significantly shaped the tech industry, such as Gmail, an email service that transformed the way people communicate, and Google Maps, which revolutionized navigation and location services. These advancements highlight the substantial benefits of investing in employee development, supporting both individuals and the organization, and reinforcing Google's status as a leader in the tech sector.

☑ **Mutual Growth Dynamics:**

- **Empowered Creativity:** Employees are given the freedom to innovate and explore.

- **Organizational Advancement:** Google benefits from breakthrough innovations and increased employee engagement.

- **Sustained Leadership:** Mutual investment creates a cycle where both employees and the organization flourish.

1.7.2 Accountability: Safeguarding Integrity and Excellence

Accountability is a fundamental element that greatly enhances relationships by ensuring they align with core values and shared objectives. It fosters an environment of transparency, allowing both parties to feel a sense of ownership over their actions and the resulting outcomes. This shared responsibility nurtures a culture of trust, enabling individuals to express their thoughts, concerns, and aspirations openly without fear of judgment or retribution.

In the context of symbiotic relationships- be they personal, professional, or collaborative- accountability serves as a crucial safeguard against complacency. It acts as a constant reminder for both parties to stay engaged and committed to their mutual growth and development, fostering active participation in the evolution of the relationship. By reinforcing ethical conduct and sound practices, accountability encourages individuals to consistently evaluate their values, motivations, and behaviors, thereby maintaining the integrity of their relationship.

Furthermore, this commitment to accountability drives a collective pursuit of excellence, encouraging each participant to strive for improvement and innovation. By holding one another accountable, individuals not only help each other realize their potential but also cultivate an environment that embraces constructive feedback and learning. Incorporating accountability into relationships leads to a more resilient and dynamic partnership, capable of adapting to challenges and thriving in changing circumstances. As individuals take responsibility for their roles and contributions, they build a stronger foundation for collaboration and success, ensuring that the relationship can endure and flourish over time.

Core Elements of Accountability:

1. **Clear Expectations:** Establishing mutually agreed-upon standards and goals.
2. **Regular Check-Ins:** Engaging in consistent communication and progress assessments.
3. **Honest Feedback:** Providing constructive input to address challenges and refine strategies.
4. **Mutual Responsibility:** Holding one another accountable for individual and collective success.

Leadership Insight:

Leaders who prioritize cultivating a culture of accountability genuinely empower their teams to take ownership of their responsibilities. This approach not only enhances individual performance but also fosters a collaborative environment where trust is deeply rooted. When leaders demonstrate transparency and integrity in their actions and decisions, they set a powerful example for their teams. Such behavior creates a framework where team members feel both encouraged and obligated to hold themselves and their colleagues accountable.

This culture encourages open communication, enabling team members to voice concerns and provide constructive feedback without fearing retribution. Consequently, employees invest more in their tasks and results, realizing that their contributions significantly influence the team's success. In the end, a robust culture of accountability results in higher engagement, better performance metrics, and a sense of fulfillment at work, as individuals see that their efforts are acknowledged and appreciated.

Case Study: The Accountability Culture at Bridgewater Associates

Bridgewater Associates, recognized as one of the largest hedge funds in the world, is noted for its unique approach to corporate culture, defined by radical transparency and a strong sense of accountability. Under the visionary leadership of founder Ray Dalio, the firm has developed an innovative system that encourages employees at all levels to engage in honest, constructive feedback, regardless of organizational hierarchy. This practice not only fosters open communication but also cultivates a culture where all voices are valued, leading to more informed and collaborative decision-making processes.

By actively promoting accountability, Bridgewater empowers its employees to take ownership of their roles and contribute to the firm's collective success. This commitment to transparency ensures that decisions are made with integrity, which builds trust among team members and enhances overall performance. The focus on continuous improvement is embedded in the organization's ethos, motivating employees to learn from their mistakes and share insights, thereby facilitating personal and professional growth. This dynamic environment not only helps Bridgewater navigate the complexities of the financial markets but also sets a standard for others in the industry to follow.

Accountability Dynamics:

- **Open Dialogue:** Employees engage in candid discussions about performance and strategy.
- **Continuous Improvement:** Constructive feedback drives innovation and refinement.
- **Organizational Trust:** A culture of transparency strengthens team cohesion and alignment.

1.7.3 The Intersection of Mutual Growth and Accountability

Mutual growth and accountability are closely linked principles that reinforce and elevate each other. Growth without accountability can lead to aimlessness and complacency, where individuals or organizations pursue expansion without self-reflection or responsibility. This approach can waste efforts and obscure direction. Conversely, accountability without growth tends to create rigidity and stagnation, confining individuals or organizations to outdated practices and hindering their ability to adapt to new challenges or opportunities.

When these two principles align, they create a dynamic climate that fosters ongoing improvement. In this environment, both individuals and organizations are motivated to pursue their goals while also being accountable for their actions and choices.

This balance encourages continuous dialogue about progress and standards, ensuring that efforts align with core values and objectives. Ultimately, the interplay between growth and accountability cultivates a resilient culture where innovation thrives and individuals feel empowered to make meaningful contributions to their collective success.

Benefits of Integrating Mutual Growth and Accountability:

- **Increased Trust:** Consistent feedback and mutual investment cultivate trust and reliability.
- **Enhanced Performance:** Individuals and teams perform at higher levels when they are supported and held accountable.
- **Resilience in Adversity:** A culture of mutual growth and accountability equips organizations to navigate challenges effectively.

Leadership Insight:

Leaders who effectively balance mutual growth with accountability cultivate high-performing teams that are not only resilient and innovative but also deeply committed to achieving shared goals. By creating an environment where each team member feels empowered to pursue personal and professional development while being held accountable for their contributions, these leaders lay a strong foundation for sustainable excellence. This approach fosters a culture of trust and collaboration, encouraging individuals to take risks and embrace new ideas. Ultimately, when team members feel supported in their growth and understand the importance of their responsibilities, they are more likely to engage fully, adapt to challenges, and contribute to a collective vision of success.

1.7.4 Consequences of Neglecting Mutual Growth and Accountability

When mutual growth and accountability are overlooked, both relationships and organizations can be vulnerable to various detrimental outcomes, including stagnation, misalignment, and, in severe cases, total failure. A strong commitment to growth is essential; without it, individuals and teams may fall into complacency, effectively stalling their progress and innovation. This complacency can suppress creativity and hinder the exploration of new ideas, ultimately obstructing both personal and collective advancement.

Moreover, the absence of accountability creates an environment in which ethical standards can deteriorate, resulting in poor decision-making becoming the norm. When team members do not hold one another accountable, the likelihood of unethical behavior increases, prompting decisions that focus on immediate gains instead of long-term growth. This unregulated atmosphere can lead to a reduction in trust and communication, exacerbating the misalignment between team members and their objectives.

Therefore, fostering a culture that prioritizes both growth and accountability is essential. This entails creating opportunities for continuous learning, encouraging open feedback, and implementing systems that reinforce ethical behavior. By doing this, individuals and organizations can cultivate resilience, adaptability, and a shared sense of purpose that paves the way for lasting success.

Consequences of Neglect:

- **Loss of Trust:** Without accountability, trust erodes, making it difficult to rebuild.
- **Stagnation and Decline:** Complacency stifles innovation and limits potential.
- **Ethical Vulnerability:** The absence of accountability increases the risk of unethical behavior and decision-making.

Case Study: Enron's Collapse Due to Lack of Accountability

The downfall of Enron Corporation serves as a significant cautionary tale highlighting the severe repercussions of poor accountability in corporate governance. At its peak, Enron was celebrated as an innovative energy firm; however, beneath this façade lay a culture rife with greed and unethical conduct. The company's leadership engaged in a systematic distortion of financial records, employing complex accounting methods such as mark-to-market accounting and special purpose entities to obscure major losses from investors and regulators.

Without a reliable accountability system, the company prioritized profits over ethical standards, leading to careless decision-making and fraudulent behavior. The consequences of these choices were catastrophic, culminating in one of the largest corporate scandals ever. Enron's bankruptcy obliterated the savings and employment of thousands, prompting a wave of regulatory reforms, including the Sarbanes-Oxley Act of 2002, aimed at enhancing transparency and accountability in financial reporting.

The Enron scandal significantly undermined public confidence in corporate America. This incident heightened skepticism regarding corporate leaders and financial institutions. It highlights the critical need for ethical standards and accountability to maintain the integrity of the corporate sector.

☑ **Consequences of Neglect Dynamics:**

- **Lack of Oversight:** The absence of accountability allowed unethical behavior to go unchecked.

- **Loss of Stakeholder Trust:** The collapse led to widespread disillusionment and financial ruin.

- **Irreparable Damage:** Enron's demise underscored the importance of accountability in sustaining trust and integrity.

1.7.5 Practical Strategies for Cultivating Mutual Growth and Accountability

Creating environments that nurture mutual growth and accountability requires a thoughtful and deliberate approach marked by intentionality, clear structures, and a steadfast commitment from all parties involved. In personal relationships, this may involve not only establishing open lines of communication but also fostering a safe space for individuals to express their thoughts and feelings freely. Setting shared goals that resonate with each person's aspirations encourages them to actively support one another's journeys, cultivating a deeper sense of partnership and collaboration. In professional relationships, fostering a culture of accountability is strengthened by consistent feedback methods, including regular performance reviews and informal check-ins, aiding in aligning expectations and acknowledging successes.

Implementing collaborative projects that embody the organization's core values not only reinforces a sense of community but also allows team members to leverage their strengths while learning from one another. Promoting transparency in decision-making processes can further empower employees and enhance their commitment to the organization's goals. Within spiritual communities, fostering an atmosphere of growth can be achieved by organizing discussions, workshops, and retreats that deepen participants' understanding of spiritual principles. These gatherings provide opportunities for collective reflection and personal development, enabling members to explore their beliefs and engage with their community on a deeper level.

Integrating these principles into daily practices- whether in personal relationships, workplaces, or community environments- helps individuals and organizations remain true to their core values. This adherence fosters a culture of mutual support and success while nurturing an ongoing commitment to excellence that benefits everyone involved. These settings excel in continuous learning, enabling individuals and groups to effectively overcome challenges while collectively celebrating their growth.

Strategies for Cultivating Mutual Growth:

1. **Set Clear Goals:** Start by collaboratively setting specific, measurable objectives that not only align with individual aspirations but also support the organization's overarching goals. Make sure these goals are communicated clearly and revisited regularly to assess progress, promoting a shared understanding of success at all levels.

2. **Encourage Continuous Learning:** Cultivate a culture that values continuous professional and personal development by offering diverse learning opportunities. This could include workshops, online courses, mentorship programs, or access to industry conferences. Encourage team members to pursue interests that enhance their skills and knowledge, ensuring they feel supported in their growth journey.

3. **Celebrate Progress:** Actively recognize and reward achievements, both large and small, to reinforce a culture of growth and motivation. Develop both formal and informal methods to celebrate milestones, such as team meetings, company newsletters, or recognition boards. This acknowledgment fosters a sense of accomplishment and encourages a positive environment where individuals feel valued for their contributions.

Strategies for Strengthening Accountability:

1. **Define Expectations Clearly:** Clearly define specific roles and responsibilities for each team member, ensuring that everyone understands their individual contributions to the overall goals of the organization. Set performance standards that are both measurable and attainable, outlining clear criteria for success. This clarity promotes a sense of ownership and accountability among team members.

2. **Establish Feedback Mechanisms:** Implement regular check-ins and structured feedback sessions, like weekly one-on-ones or monthly performance reviews, to promote open communication. During these sessions, provide constructive feedback that highlights strengths and areas for improvement, cultivating a growth

mindset. Additionally, encourage team members to share their thoughts and insights to create a two-way feedback loop that enhances team collaboration.

3. **Model Accountability:** As a leader, show transparency and ethical behavior in everything you do, establishing a strong standard of integrity and responsibility for the team. Recognize your mistakes and learn from them, emphasizing that accountability is a shared commitment. By consistently embodying these values, you foster a culture of trust and respect, inspiring others to do the same in their roles.

Conclusion: The Power of Mutual Growth and Accountability

Mutual growth and accountability are the foundation of strong, symbiotic relationships, essential for success in both personal and professional contexts. These principles ensure that individuals, teams, and organizations align with their core values while striving for continuous improvement. By actively investing in one another's development, through mentorship, knowledge sharing, or constructive feedback, we foster an environment that promotes trust and collaboration.

Equally important is our commitment to holding each other accountable. This sense of accountability fosters a culture of responsibility and openness, empowering individuals to meet their obligations and achieve shared objectives. By collaborating to support one another's growth and maintain high standards, we cultivate vibrant ecosystems where excellence thrives, and long-term success becomes a certainty rather than a mere possibility. In these environments, we can tackle challenges more effectively, innovate confidently, and achieve a greater collective impact.

Chapter 1 Recap: The Importance of Symbiosis in Modern Relationships

In wrapping up our exploration of symbiosis, it's clear that this concept goes beyond its biological roots, reaching into the essence of meaningful human relationships and effective leadership. Symbiosis extends beyond mere cooperation; it serves as a vital framework that sheds light on how individuals, teams, and whole communities thrive through principles of mutual benefit, accountability, and a collective sense of purpose.

At its core, symbiosis emphasizes the mutuality of relationships, illustrating that true success is often achieved through collaboration rather than competition. When individuals and organizations recognize the importance of working together, leveraging each other's strengths, and addressing weaknesses, they foster environments where creativity and innovation can thrive. This interconnectedness nurtures a culture of trust and resilience, where members feel valued and empowered to contribute.

Moreover, the essence of symbiosis influences leadership, as effective leaders exemplify mutual respect and shared goals. They inspire their teams by cultivating a vision that aligns personal ambitions with group objectives, enabling everyone to work toward a common purpose. These leaders understand that accountability runs both ways, fostering responsibility among team members and a commitment to support and uplift those they guide.

Ultimately, embracing symbiosis in our personal or professional relationships enriches our interactions and fosters sustainable growth. By nurturing connections built on collaboration, empathy, and shared purpose, we can create vibrant communities that survive and thrive in an increasingly complex world. This chapter examines symbiosis through multiple lenses: historical, relational, cosmic, and spiritual, highlighting its importance for human well-being throughout time and space. The results suggest that interdependence fosters sustainability, resilience, and growth in nature, the universe, and leadership.

Let's reflect on some of the most important insights from this chapter and how they relate to leadership today:

🔄 Historical Roots & Human Legacy

Historically, partnerships have been essential in shaping societies. These relationships reveal an important truth: the strongest and most enduring connections are founded on interdependence and common objectives. Within these partnerships, leaders cultivate a cooperative spirit where success is attained through mutual investment, trust, and shared accountability. The essence of effective leadership lies not in isolation but in the ability to draw upon the strengths of others, recognizing that collective effort often leads to greater innovation and resilience. Whether in small communities or at the international level, these enduring bonds remind us that collaboration is vital for overcoming challenges and achieving common aspirations.

☑ Leadership Parallel:

Effective leaders understand that their team's greatest strength does not come from dominating others but from encouraging teamwork. They recognize the value of diverse perspectives and talents, acknowledging that success cannot be achieved by one person alone. Building partnerships creates an environment where everyone feels valued and empowered, ultimately improving the team's overall strength. This approach nurtures trust and open communication, sparks creativity and innovation, and nurtures a sense of unity and shared purpose among all team members.

🌏 Nature and the Universe as Our Blueprint

Nature's ecosystems and the complex cosmic interactions in the universe convey a deep truth: All life thrives through interconnectedness, not isolation. Take the fascinating relationship between fungi and trees. Fungi create underground networks that facilitate nutrient exchange, benefiting both themselves and the trees. This mutualism not only boosts growth but also strengthens the entire ecosystem.

Additionally, the Earth's connection with the Sun illustrates a further aspect of this interconnectedness. The Sun delivers essential energy that fuels photosynthesis in plants, which, in turn, generate oxygen and organic matter vital for the survival of numerous species. This intricate balance and mutual contribution emphasize that life is a tapestry crafted from various threads that are each dependent on the others for nourishment and survival.

In broader terms, these interactions remind us that harmony in nature requires cooperation, mutual support, and understanding. When elements work in concert, whether in an ecosystem or within the cosmos, they create conditions where life can truly thrive. Emphasizing this interconnectedness encourages us to appreciate our role within a larger community, urging us to nurture these relationships for future generations.

✅ Leadership Parallel:

Leaders are most effective when they create environments grounded in trust, creativity, and collaboration. These environments resemble thriving ecosystems that nurture and sustain life, prioritizing cooperation over competition. By promoting open communication and welcoming diverse viewpoints, leaders can stimulate innovative thinking and collaborative problem-solving. In such settings, individuals feel valued and empowered to share their ideas, fostering a more cohesive and dynamic team. Ultimately, the strength of these ecological networks lies in their ability to adapt and evolve together, ensuring lasting success for the entire organization.

🐚 The Power of Reciprocity

Healthy relationships thrive on a continuous exchange of giving and receiving, ensuring that both individuals feel appreciated and supported. This concept not only pertains to personal relationships but also applies to organizational contexts such as businesses, families, and ministries. When reciprocal investment becomes the norm rather than an infrequent event, a vibrant dynamic starts to flourish.

From a business standpoint, companies that promote mutual support among employees through encouragement of feedback, collaboration, and mentorship often cultivate a more engaged and productive workforce. In a similar vein, in family dynamics, maintaining open communication and shared responsibilities fosters a nurturing atmosphere where every member feels empowered and connected. Moreover, prioritizing shared investment nurtures a strong sense of community. When leaders and members participate together through service, shared objectives, and open communication, it results in a more vibrant and resilient congregation. Ultimately, the health of any relationship, whether personal or organizational, relies on the fundamental practice of giving and receiving, creating a balanced harmony that benefits everyone.

Leadership Parallel:

Leaders who actively invest in their teams by advancing a culture of encouragement, recognition, and growth opportunities tend to reap significant rewards in employee commitment, innovation, and sustained success. By offering regular encouragement, leaders not only motivate their employees but also create an environment where individuals feel valued and understood. Recognition, whether through formal awards or simple gestures of appreciation, boosts morale and reinforces positive behaviors.

Additionally, providing professional development opportunities such as training programs, mentorship, and career advancement paths empowers employees to hone their skills and contribute creatively to the organization. This holistic approach enhances individual performance and cultivates a loyal workforce eager to overcome challenges and drive the organization toward long-term achievements.

Avoiding Parasitism and Exploitation

In our examination of the mechanics of symbiosis, we explored the counterforces that disrupt this harmonious relationship, focusing on parasitism, manipulation, and unchecked competition. Parasitism occurs when one party benefits at the expense of another, leading to exploitation that can severely undermine the health of the entire system. Manipulation involves one entity leveraging its influence to control or exploit the actions of another, creating a power imbalance that erodes trust. Additionally, unchecked competition can create an environment where individuals or groups prioritize their own success over collaboration, resulting in burnout and diminishing returns for everyone involved. These imbalances not only threaten the stability of relationships but also fracture the fundamental trust that is essential for any cooperative endeavor to thrive.

Leadership Parallel:

Effective leaders possess the insight to identify when relationships become one-sided or turn toxic. They do not hesitate to confront situations of exploitation, whether it manifests as an imbalance in contributions, emotional manipulation, or a lack of mutual respect. Recognizing these patterns is crucial for maintaining the integrity of their interactions. When noticing these unhealthy patterns, wise leaders take proactive steps to correct them. This may involve initiating difficult conversations, providing constructive feedback, or modifying expectations and responsibilities. They recognize the significance of establishing clear boundaries that protect not only their own well-being but also that of others involved. By doing so, they promote a culture of respect and support, ensuring that relationships are marked by mutual benefit and understanding. This dedication to healthy relational dynamics ultimately fosters a more positive and productive environment for everyone.

☑ **Leadership Parallel:**

Effective leadership is fundamentally grounded in the principles of humility and service, highlighting the importance of empowering others to achieve their potential. This leadership approach emphasizes deep respect for the inherent value of each individual, fostering an environment where collaboration and support can flourish. By prioritizing the needs of team members and encouraging their development, leaders create a culture that champions ethical conduct and shared success. Ultimately, this leadership model mirrors the best practices for building harmonious relationships and collective prosperity within organizations.

Looking Ahead: Applying Symbiosis to Every Relationship

As we now turn the page to Chapter 2: The Different Types of Relationships, we will apply these symbiotic principles to various relational contexts: family, friendship, love, professional connections, and more. You will see how the nature of reciprocity, accountability, growth, and shared purpose differ in each relationship, yet remain equally vital. Symbiosis is not a distant concept; it is a daily calling, an invitation to lead, love, and live in a way that enables both you and those around you to thrive together. 🌱 ✻

CHAPTER 2
The Different Types of Relationships

Chapter 2: The Different Types of Relationships

Symbiosis in human interaction takes on various forms, shaped by the unique characteristics of each relationship. At the core of these relationships are fundamental principles such as mutual benefit, trust, accountability, and growth. While these principles are universally applicable, their expressions differ significantly based on the context. Whether we navigate the complexities of family dynamics, foster bonds within friendships, nurture romantic partnerships, or collaborate in professional teams, the vitality of each relationship is ultimately determined by how well we recognize, respect, and cultivate interdependence.

Gaining a deep understanding of relational connections in various settings is essential for promoting intentional leadership, enhancing love, and building lasting relationships. For instance, in a family, fostering open communication and shared experiences can strengthen trust and support. In friendships, creating a space for vulnerability and consistently offering support encourages mutual development. Romantic relationships flourish through emotional intimacy and shared objectives, while professional interactions thrive on clear accountability and a unifying vision.

This chapter explores the fundamental types of relationships, highlighting their distinctive characteristics and challenges. It draws upon leadership principles and biblical teachings to shed light on ways to strengthen these connections and improve their effectiveness. By examining these concepts in greater depth, we can acquire insights into creating environments that nurture thriving relationships, ultimately improving our lives and those of others around us.

2.1 Family: The First Environment for Symbiosis

Family is often our first encounter with the concept of human connection, serving as a crucial foundation for all our future relationships. Within this intimate unit, we observe and experience the principles of symbiosis, which can either flourish or be absent altogether. The family environment plays a vital role in shaping our core values, influencing our identities, and laying the emotional groundwork that will support us throughout our lives.

In an ideal scenario, families function as nurturing ecosystems, fostering not only support and accountability but also encouraging personal growth and offering unconditional love. Healthy family dynamics showcase the essence of symbiosis, illustrating a harmonious exchange where each member contributes to and draws from the collective well-being of the family. These relationships are characterized by empathy, mutual respect, and a shared commitment to each other's development, creating a safe haven where individuals can thrive together.

2.1.1 Mutual Contribution in Family Relationships

In a symbiotic family, every member contributes uniquely, strengthening the overall harmony and well-being of the group. Parents play a vital role in offering care, structure, and guidance, advancing a nurturing atmosphere for children's growth and development. They instill important values like respect, empathy, and perseverance while also equipping their children with practical life skills essential for facing real-world challenges. This supportive framework shapes children's understanding of the world and fosters strong emotional bonds, ensuring the family unit thrives together in a mutually beneficial relationship.

Children bring new viewpoints, endless enthusiasm, and a revitalized sense of purpose to family life. Their natural curiosity drives them to investigate their surroundings, often sparking imaginative play and inventive solutions that parents might have overlooked. This lively energy not only fills the household with joy and movement but also encourages parents to appreciate life's little joys.

When children share their discoveries with adults- from small insects to the intricate changes of the seasons- they open parents' eyes to the remarkable things hidden in everyday life. This helps to reignite a sense of joy and wonder that often diminishes with adult responsibilities. Thus, children inspire a greater appreciation for daily experiences, motivating families to treasure their moments together and to perceive the world with curiosity and enthusiasm.

Siblings hold a unique and intricately linked position in each other's lives, acting as both spirited rivals and loyal supporters. Their interactions, rich in playful competition and affectionate teasing, create an essential basis for personal growth. Through playful disagreements and active contests, they engage in a lively interaction that sharpens essential life skills such as negotiation, clear communication, and the subtle art of collaboration.

Sibling relationships nurture a profound sense of loyalty as they often become each other's staunchest allies during challenging times. They learn to navigate the turbulent waters of conflict, cultivating a deeper understanding of empathy and the subtleties of compromise with each disagreement. This ongoing experience fosters the vital skill of forgiveness, enabling them to mend rifts and strengthen their bond. As they enthusiastically celebrate one another's achievements, whether academic milestones, athletic victories, or personal triumphs, siblings create and advance a supportive atmosphere that encourages both individual growth and collective pride. Over time, these shared experiences weave together to create a resilient connection that often lasts into adulthood, providing a lasting source of strength, unwavering love, and cherished companionship throughout life's myriad challenges and jubilations.

Together, these varied contributions create a rich tapestry of interdependence, where each family member's strengths and weaknesses are acknowledged and embraced, leading to a more profound understanding of love, resilience, and cooperation.

☑ Leadership Parallel:

Leaders within a family, usually the parents or guardians, face the important challenge of balancing authority with humility and discipline with compassion. These family leaders exemplify the principles of servant leadership by putting the needs of the family members above their own. They lead by example, showcasing behaviors and values they wish to instill in their children. This approach creates an environment where each family member feels valued and supported, fostering personal growth and self-discovery.

Moreover, effective family leaders hold themselves accountable to the family's core values, consistently reflecting on their decisions and actions to ensure they align with the principles they teach. This commitment builds trust among family members and establishes a strong foundation for open communication and mutual respect. By nurturing a sense of unity and shared purpose, family leaders foster a thriving household where everyone is empowered to reach their full potential.

2.1.2 Reciprocity and Respect Across Generations

Respect within the parent-child relationship should be a two-way street. That means thriving through mutual appreciation and understanding. While children are taught to honor their parents, it is equally important for parents to respond with dignity, gentleness, and respect toward their children. This reciprocal relationship fosters an environment in which emotional investment, forgiveness, and care are not just expected but actively practiced by both parties. By nurturing these qualities, families can strengthen their generational bonds and create a legacy of compassion and support that transcends age and experience. This framework lays the foundation for healthier communication, deeper trust, and enhanced emotional resilience within the family unit.

Building on this foundation, active listening and open communication are crucial for fostering respect in the parent-child relationship. When parents make a conscious effort to genuinely listen to their children's thoughts and feelings, it validates their experiences and emotions, cultivating a sense of belonging and worth. Conversely, when children observe their parents thoughtfully engaging with their concerns and opinions, it instills confidence and encourages them to express themselves openly.

In addition to fostering a sense of security, setting boundaries helps children develop self-discipline and decision-making skills. When children understand the expectations established by their parents, they are more likely to make choices that align with those guidelines. This not only encourages positive behavior but also cultivates a sense of responsibility as they learn to navigate their environment within the defined limits.

Moreover, boundaries give parents a framework for consistency, reinforcing their role as caregivers and guides. This structured approach helps reduce conflicts and misunderstandings, leading to healthier parent-child relationships where open communication thrives. In the end, established boundaries are not just guidelines; they are vital instruments for fostering growth and promoting mutual respect within the family structure.

Recognizing and celebrating each other's achievements, regardless of their size, plays a crucial role in fostering a culture of mutual appreciation and support within a family. This practice not only enhances self-esteem for everyone involved but also creates an environment where individuals feel valued and understood. When family members consistently acknowledge one another's successes, whether it's a child mastering a new skill, an adult achieving a professional milestone, or simply showing kindness, these moments of recognition contribute to building a strong, resilient family dynamic. Over time, such positive reinforcement cultivates a sense of belonging and empowerment that resonates deeply within each member.

The nurturing atmosphere within the family promotes values of recognition and appreciation. As individuals carry these values into their interactions with friends and colleagues, they tend to replicate the supportive behaviors learned at home. This not only enhances their social interactions but also cultivates healthier and more positive relationships in all aspects of their lives.

☑ **Leadership Parallel:**

Strong family leadership cultivates a space where open communication can flow, making every member feel appreciated and acknowledged. In this environment, feedback is embraced and sought after, fostering a culture of trust and teamwork. Leaders focus on the well-being of the family as a whole when making choices, considering the varied perspectives and needs of each member. This inclusive method not only enhances family connections but also empowers individuals to engage meaningfully, resulting in healthier and more vibrant family relationships.

2.1.3 Accountability and Grace in Family Structures

Accountability within a family is a fundamental principle that encompasses a variety of important practices. It involves not only keeping promises and honoring commitments but also acknowledging mistakes and taking responsibility for one's actions. This process is essential for fostering a culture of honesty and openness, where members feel safe to express their feelings and concerns.

When accountability is embraced within a family, it acts as a powerful tool to prevent the unsettling drift into dysfunction. This dysfunction often manifests through negative behaviors such as resentment, withdrawal, and silence among family members, creating an emotional chasm. Over time, this negativity can erode the bonds that hold relationships together, resulting in misunderstandings and a profound lack of connection.

However, when accountability is paired with grace, an attitude of compassion and forgiveness, it transforms into a powerful, refining force. This combination helps strengthen trust as families learn to navigate their challenges together, supporting one another through difficulties while holding each other accountable. By fostering an environment where accountability and grace coexist, families can cultivate deeper emotional bonds and a more resilient, harmonious atmosphere.

By fostering a culture of accountability, family members can express their thoughts and feelings openly, which cultivates trust and understanding. This proactive approach not only addresses issues as they arise but also encourages individuals to take responsibility for their actions and their impact on others. As a result, families can build a stronger foundation of communication and support, ultimately enhancing their emotional intimacy and resilience against potential conflicts.

✅ Leadership Parallel:

Effective leaders, like caring and attentive parents, understand the value of admitting their mistakes. They readily acknowledge when they are wrong, reflecting a desire to learn and develop from their experiences. By demonstrating true remorse and atonement, they illustrate that making mistakes is acceptable and crucial to owning one's actions.

Furthermore, these leaders cultivate a culture of mutual accountability by encouraging their teams or families to share the responsibility for collective outcomes. Trust is established not on the illusion of perfection but on a foundation of consistency and humility. They tackle challenges with an open heart, consistently valuing the input of others while remaining grounded in their principles. Engaging in these practices fosters an environment where collaboration flourishes, allowing individuals to bring forth their best selves.

At the same time, accountability builds trust and responsibility, prompting individuals to acknowledge their actions and their effects on others. These elements work together to support a balanced environment that allows open communication to thrive, conflicts to be resolved positively, and robust, supportive relationships to develop over time. By embracing both forgiveness and accountability, we not only fortify family connections but also establish a foundation for nurturing and flexible relationships.

2.1.4 When Symbiosis Breaks Down: Family Disintegration

When family relationships become unbalanced due to favoritism, neglect, or unresolved trauma, they can easily turn toxic. This shift often leads to a state of silence and bitterness, where manipulation becomes prevalent. As a result, open communication is stifled, leaving family members feeling alienated and resentful.

If left unaddressed, relational breakdowns can become ingrained over time, affecting multiple generations and continuing cycles of emotional distress and dysfunction. The lack of empathetic communication and mutual understanding can lead to significant cracks in family relationships, complicating individuals' ability to handle these complexities independently. To heal these wounds, it is essential to recognize the present issues and commit to nurturing healthier interactions and restoring trust within the family.

☑ **Leadership Application:**

Acknowledging and addressing imbalances within family dynamics is the crucial first step toward achieving restoration and harmony. Family leaders- whether parents, guardians, or elder siblings- play a vital role in this process. It is essential for them to adopt a proactive approach by clearly defining and enforcing healthy boundaries that promote both individual and collective well-being.

This involves identifying areas of conflict or misunderstanding and actively seeking healing through open communication and conflict resolution strategies. Furthermore, reestablishing a foundation of mutual respect is crucial, as it nurtures a supportive environment where each member feels valued and heard. By prioritizing these actions, families can progress toward a more balanced and harmonious relationship.

Chapter 2.1 Summary: Family – The First Environment for Symbiosis

The family unit is the first and most formative environment where the principles of symbiosis are either nurtured or neglected. It is within this foundational space that individuals first learn to give and receive, to grow and be accountable, and to lead with both strength and grace. When functioning properly, a family reflects a powerful model of interdependence, emotional safety, and unconditional support, qualities that form the foundation of all future relationships.

In this section, we examined how mutual contribution, reciprocity, accountability, and empathy influence the dynamics of strong families. Parents act as servant-leaders, providing guidance through consistent love, humility, and discipline. Children, in turn, contribute curiosity, energy, and a fresh perspective, while siblings provide lifelong opportunities to develop communication skills, loyalty, and the ability to resolve conflicts with grace.

Families that focus on shared growth and accountability demonstrate greater resilience when confronting life's challenges. By fostering open communication, establishing healthy boundaries, and celebrating each other's successes, these familial ties are reinforced. Consequently, family members build enduring relationships that continue to flourish into adulthood.

When symbiosis is disturbed by favoritism, emotional neglect, manipulation, or unresolved trauma, relationships face the danger of slipping into cycles of resentment and dysfunction. However, even amid breakdown, there is still a chance for restoration. By practicing intentional leadership, setting clear boundaries, and dedicating themselves to healing, families can restore trust and reestablish their symbiotic harmony.

Leadership Parallels Recap:

- **Family leaders serve like transformational leaders**, modeling humility, vision, and empathy while guiding the household toward shared values.
- **Healthy family leadership mirrors servant leadership**, where those in authority lift others up rather than dominate.

- **Accountable leadership at home builds trust**, encourages emotional transparency, and nurtures individual growth.

Visionary leadership steps in to heal dysfunction, identifying root issues, reinforcing boundaries, and restoring relational balance.

⚜ Final Thought:

The family serves as our primary environment for learning and developing relational skills. It shapes our understanding of interpersonal dynamics and lays the foundation for how we engage with others throughout our lives. The values, communication styles, and conflict resolution strategies we observe and practice in the family setting often become the blueprint for our interactions in friendships, romantic relationships, and professional environments.

By encouraging a culture of collaboration, support, and open dialogue at home, we nurture our personal growth and empower our loved ones to develop essential qualities such as emotional intelligence, resilience, and effective leadership. These interconnected principles advance a deep sense of connection and mutual understanding, allowing us to navigate challenges and cultivate strong, healthy relationships in all aspects of life. Ultimately, the skills and emotional resources nurtured within the family unit play a vital role in our ability to flourish in all areas of life, enabling us to make positive contributions to our communities and workplaces.

2.2 Friendship: A Chosen Symbiotic Relationship

Family certainly sets the stage for important relationship skills, but it is often in our friendships that we truly explore, deepen, and refine those lessons. Unlike family ties that occur naturally through birth or circumstance, friendships are special bonds we choose, built on shared values, mutual respect, and a sincere connection. These relationships flourish because we select our friends based on what resonates with us and what we enjoy together, giving them a personal and unique touch.

Friendship creates a foundation for symbiosis to flourish, providing a nurturing space where mutual growth and support can truly thrive. Unlike family relationships, which sometimes feel connected by obligation or circumstance, friendships are built through a conscious choice to connect. This beautiful aspect of voluntary connection enables individuals to cultivate deep, meaningful bonds filled with trust, encouragement, shared accountability, and a wonderful mix of collective experiences.

In this treasured sphere of friendship, the interactions sharply contrast with family relationships. Unlike family ties, which often involve fixed roles, friendships necessitate continuous attention and cultivation. They call for a commitment to intentional reciprocity, with both individuals actively participating in the exchange of support. This emotional transparency fosters a safe space for vulnerability, enabling friends to express their authentic selves without the fear of criticism.

In this section, we will examine how symbiosis principles appear in friendships, showcasing how mutual investment, steadfast loyalty, and a sense of accountability can turn casual acquaintances into meaningful relationships. We will analyze the dynamics of reciprocity, where both parties contribute to and gain from the relationship, creating a sense of belonging and support. By recognizing these factors, we can see how friendships enrich our lives and act as significant drivers of personal growth, resilience, and emotional health.

2.2.1 The Power of Mutual Investment

Symbiotic friendships flourish when both individuals actively engage in supporting each other's well-being and personal growth. Unlike transactional relationships, which often revolve around a give-and-take mentality, these deep connections are built on the foundation of genuine partnership and mutual investment. They are characterized by consistent encouragement, unwavering companionship, and steadfast support, creating an environment where each person feels valued and understood.

In such enriching friendships, each individual serves as a source of inspiration for the other, motivating them to strive for their best selves. This reciprocal influence fosters a continuous cycle of growth and self-improvement, where both friends celebrate achievements and navigate challenges together. They create a safe haven, a nurturing space that embraces vulnerability, allowing each person to share their fears, insecurities, and aspirations openly without judgment.

The caring environment promotes healing and strengthens their bond, creating a crucial safe haven for emotional exploration. Within this encouraging space, they can engage in meaningful conversations that deepen their understanding of each other. Through these profound exchanges, both friends experience growth in self-awareness and resilience. Ultimately, these mutually supportive friendships enrich their lives by nurturing a profound sense of belonging and shared aspirations. They elevate each person's journey, easing burdens and amplifying joys as both friends journey alongside each other in their quests for fulfillment and happiness.

✅ Leadership Parallel:

Strong friendships, similar to effective peer leadership, are founded on qualities like emotional intelligence, empathy, and active listening. These traits create understanding and closeness, enabling friends to face challenges together. Instead of exercising authority, friends influence one another through shared experiences and mutual respect, fostering a collaborative and supportive environment. This relationship promotes accountability, empowering individuals to encourage each other while also holding one another accountable during tough times. In essence, the power of a friendship resides in its ability to uplift and motivate each other, strengthening bonds rooted in trust and open communication.

2.2.2 Reciprocity in Emotional Support

In healthy friendships, a lively and supportive exchange occurs between people, providing emotional, mental, and spiritual backing that benefits both. This give-and-take relationship features a balance of attentive listening, sincere encouragement, insightful advice, and genuine celebration of each other's achievements and milestones. In these interactions, both individuals feel deeply appreciated and uplifted, creating a space where they can thrive and develop their true selves.

However, when this delicate balance tilts too far in one direction, such as when one individual becomes overly reliant on the other for emotional support or begins to monopolize conversations, friendships can shift from being invigorating to exhausting. Instead of fostering a deep sense of vitality and connection, these relationships can devolve into transactional exchanges, where interactions prioritize completing tasks or obligations over genuine, meaningful engagement. This shift can lead to feelings of frustration and resentment, eroding the foundation of trust and support that initially defined the friendship.

It is crucial for both individuals to stay vigilant and dedicated to maintaining this balance. Open communication is vital, as discussing feelings of imbalance- whether related to emotional dependency or conversational dominance- can aid in restoring harmony. By actively investing time and effort into nurturing their connection, friends can develop relationships that are truly life-enhancing, rewarding, and enriching for both parties. Ultimately, it is this balance that turns casual acquaintances into valued companions who support each other through life's ups and downs.

✅ Leadership Parallel:

Reciprocity in leadership resembles mentorship, evolving into a mutual exchange. This concept extends beyond the traditional view of a leader imparting knowledge to their followers. It emphasizes the significance of a two-way relationship where both individuals contribute to each other's growth. Even when one person possesses more experience or authority, nurturing a reciprocal dynamic promotes shared learning and fosters respect and trust.

In friendships, reciprocity deepens, characterized by shared emotional support and a mutual willingness to be vulnerable. Each person contributes to the other's well-being, creating a secure environment for open communication and support. This give-and-take not only strengthens the relationship but also encourages personal growth and resilience. Ultimately, this mutual exchange enhances both leadership and personal connections, leading to more meaningful experiences and a deeper understanding.

Modern Example:

The lasting bond between Oprah Winfrey and Gayle King exemplifies the power of mutual support in both personal and professional settings. Throughout the years, they have weathered life's ups and downs, from major obstacles to great successes, always being there for one another. Their relationship illustrates that the foundation of lasting bonds lies in shared experiences, open communication, and unwavering encouragement. Through times of joy and difficulty, Oprah and Gayle have demonstrated that investing in one another not only strengthens trust but also fosters individual growth. Their wonderful collaboration beautifully shows how deep and trusting friendships can grow and thrive, enriching not only their lives but also the lives of everyone around them.

2.2.3 Accountability Among Peers

True friends go beyond just offering support; they encourage each other to grow and develop. They deliver honest feedback, sharing insights that can be tough to hear yet stem from love and a sincere wish for one another's happiness. Such communication creates a space where difficult truths can be shared without the fear of judgment.

Moreover, genuine friends hold each other accountable for their values and ambitions, helping ensure they remain true to their goals and cherished principles. When friends motivate one another to pursue higher standards, it signifies a deep trust, fostering a relationship founded on mutual respect and understanding rather than simple criticism. This dynamic promotes personal growth, with each friend acting as a catalyst for the other's potential, ultimately reinforcing their bond.

Leadership Parallel:

Peer-level accountability is often overlooked as a valuable form of leadership within our workplaces and communities. Leaders who seek and value honest feedback from reliable colleagues demonstrate humility and strong self-confidence. This willingness to engage promotes a culture of trust and transparency, facilitating constructive conversations that enhance performance and build stronger relationships.

Similarly, friendships that encourage open and honest communication greatly enhance personal growth and development. Friends who feel empowered to share the truth create an environment where individuals can reflect on their actions and perspectives without the fear of judgment. When expressed thoughtfully, this honesty can serve as a powerful catalyst for transformation, motivating each person to strive for their best selves while supporting each other's journeys. In both leadership and friendship, the willingness to hold one another accountable promotes meaningful growth and a deeper understanding of each other.

2.2.4 Loyalty and Consistency Over Time

Symbiotic friendships grow over time, strengthened by a blend of shared experiences, regular interactions, and unwavering loyalty. Although an initial spark can ignite a connection, it is the continual presence and support that fosters trust over time. Friends who support each other through life's transitions, challenges, and personal changes become vital anchors in the turbulent waters of life. These lasting connections offer both stability and encourage resilience and growth, enabling individuals to thrive independently while being profoundly supported by one another. Throughout life's ups and downs, these friendships nurture a deep understanding and appreciation, showcasing the beauty of companionship that endures through time.

✅ Leadership Parallel:

Great leaders recognize the importance of cultivating long-term, loyal partnerships rather than pursuing short-lived alliances that might offer immediate benefits but lack depth. This loyalty is not just a mere expectation; it's an essential ingredient that cultivates trust among individuals and teams. When trust exists, a strong sense of psychological safety emerges—a space where people feel secure to express their ideas, take risks, and contribute fully without fear of judgment or failure.

In the context of friendship, this same loyalty serves as a solid relational foundation, like the roots of a sturdy tree that can withstand life's inevitable storms. It creates an environment where both parties can rely on one another, navigate challenges together, and celebrate successes. Such enduring connections are built over time through shared experiences, mutual support, and open communication, enabling individuals to thrive personally and professionally. Ultimately, both in leadership and friendship, the commitment to long-term loyalty fosters resilience, collaboration, and growth.

Historic Example:

The friendship shared by C.S. Lewis and J.R.R. Tolkien played a crucial role in shaping their literary works and spiritual journeys. As major figures in 20th-century literature, both authors engaged in a vibrant dialogue, critiquing each other's writings and providing support during critical phases of their careers. This camaraderie not only enhanced their writing abilities but also led to significant changes in their theological views. Their discussions, often centered on faith, mythology, and morality, helped forge a unique connection that illustrated the transformative influence of steadfast, honest friendship. Their lasting relationship influenced their own works, such as Lewis's The Chronicles of Narnia and Tolkien's The Lord of the Rings, while also leaving an indelible mark on the literary landscape, demonstrating how genuine friendship can inspire creativity and spiritual growth through the decades.

2.2.5 When Friendship Becomes Parasitic

Not all friendships are built on a foundation of mutual benefit, and this disparity can often lead to imbalanced relationships where one person consistently gives more than they receive. Such dynamics frequently give rise to one-sided friendships characterized by manipulation, in which one individual may subtly exploit the other's kindness or emotional dependency. This exploitation transforms the relationship into a toxic environment that undermines the genuine connection that should exist between friends.

When one friend routinely takes more than they give, they often disregard the essential boundaries that sustain healthy interactions. This disregard can gradually erode trust and respect, which are vital for maintaining a strong bond. Moreover, when the balance shifts, and one friend withdraws their support during challenging times- whether due to apathy, a lack of empathy, or even self-interest- it starkly reveals a fundamental lack of investment in the relationship. This withdrawal can feel like abandonment during moments of vulnerability, intensifying feelings of isolation and neglect.

As these patterns persist, they can poison the friendship, leading to growing resentment, emotional turmoil, and an eventual breakdown of what was once a meaningful connection. It's not uncommon for feelings of frustration to accumulate, leaving the more giving friend questioning their worth and the validity of the friendship itself. Recognizing and addressing these unbalanced dynamics is crucial for restoring equilibrium. Open and honest communication about expectations and boundaries can foster a healthier, more equitable friendship, allowing both individuals to nurture a supportive and reciprocal bond that enriches their lives.

Relational Red Flag:

When you often feel exhausted, overlooked, or undervalued after spending time with a friend, it suggests that the dynamics of the relationship may have shifted. This ongoing sense of emotional depletion could indicate that the connection is no longer mutual or reciprocal. Healthy friendships thrive on a foundation of support, respect, and understanding, where both parties feel heard and valued. If you notice a pattern in which your contributions and feelings are consistently disregarded or downplayed, it may be time to reflect on the relationship and consider whether it continues to serve your emotional well-being. Recognizing these signs is crucial for prioritizing your mental health and fostering relationships that uplift and inspire you rather than drain your energy.

☑ Leadership Application:

Organizational leaders often find themselves in the critical position of addressing toxic behaviors within their teams before these negative influences take root and spread. Likewise, people should identify and address toxic friendships to protect their emotional health. This proactive strategy demands self-awareness and a readiness to assess how relationships affect one's life.

Setting clear boundaries is essential; it establishes a framework for interactions that encourages respect and support. Honest conversations about feelings and expectations can also play a crucial role in transforming the relationship or determining its future. In some cases, stepping away from a friendship that consistently undermines one's self-esteem or happiness may be the most courageous and necessary act of self-leadership. By prioritizing emotional health and taking decisive action, individuals can create a more positive and supportive social environment for themselves.

Chapter 2.2 Summary: Friendship - A Chosen Symbiotic Relationship

Genuine friendship demonstrates a deep emotional and spiritual connection characterized by shared support, openness, and motivation.

- True friendship is a heartfelt connection that enriches our lives with support and understanding. It thrives through mutual encouragement, where each person feels safe to share fears and joys. This bond fosters a warm atmosphere, allowing friends to grow together, drawing strength from shared experiences and commitment.

Reciprocity is vital, as both giving and receiving nurture connection and trust.

- Reciprocity fosters meaningful relationships by nurturing connections and trust through giving and receiving. Sharing resources, support, or affection enhances our mutual understanding and appreciation. This exchange not only strengthens our ties but also creates a space for vulnerability and authenticity. Ultimately, these positive interactions establish a foundation of trust that enriches our relationships.

Accountability enhances the bond and ensures friends remain aligned with their purpose.

- Accepting accountability in love enhances the connection between individuals, nurturing a relationship based on trust and mutual respect. This commitment to being responsible to each other not only strengthens their bond but also keeps friends aligned with their common goals and ambitions, creating a strong synergy that enriches their shared journey.

Loyalty and time enhance trust, creating relationships that provide safety and renewal.

- Over time, loyalty builds trust and nurtures relationships that provide a strong sense of safety and renewal. This lasting commitment not only reinforces bonds but also creates an atmosphere where individuals feel secure and revitalized, allowing for personal growth and meaningful connections.

Recognizing imbalances safeguards emotional well-being and aids in redefining or letting go of toxic friendships.

- Recognizing emotional imbalances is essential for protecting our well-being. It enables us to evaluate our relationships critically, allowing for the possibility of redefining or even letting go of friendships that have become toxic. By acknowledging these unhealthy dynamics, we make room for healthier connections that nourish our spirit and foster personal growth.

🔑 **Leadership Takeaway:**

Just as effective leaders benefit from trusted allies and accountability partners who challenge and uplift them, individuals flourish in environments enriched by supportive friendships. These intentionally formed connections create spaces where personal growth, courage, and authentic joy can thrive. Similar to the most successful leadership teams, the best friendships foster a nurturing environment that enhances the well-being of those directly involved and positively impacts their wider social circles. These relationships promote open communication, shared vulnerability, and collective joy, ultimately strengthening trust and resilience amid life's difficulties. Such bonds, grounded in mutual respect and encouragement, are crucial for thriving both individually and as a community.

2.3 Love/Partnerships: Building Covenant through Symbiosis

While friendships are powerful choices, romantic relationships enhance that choice through deeper emotional vulnerability, exclusivity, and long-term commitment. A romantic or partnered relationship, at its best, is a symbiotic covenant built on the foundations of friendship, a shared vision, and mutual growth. When love evolves from mere emotional attraction into a purposeful partnership, it becomes a transformative bond that not only enriches the individuals involved but also establishes a stable foundation for family, community, and generational legacy.

Romantic partnerships are among the most emotionally intense human relationships, relying on mutual commitment, spiritual unity, emotional safety, and shared purpose. When two individuals choose to intertwine their lives, they create a profound connection marked by intimacy and accountability. This unique bond often leads to personal growth that is unparalleled by other types of relationships.

This strong connection creates a space for individuals to explore their vulnerabilities, develop their identities, and support one another in facing life's challenges. However, this profound potential for connection also carries significant risks. The depth of emotional involvement requires balance, empathy, and mutual support; without these essential components, a once-flourishing relationship can rapidly become a source of distress and conflict.

As empathy fades and communication breaks down, the previously harmonious bond between partners can slowly evolve into a deeply strained relationship. Navigating the complex layers of romantic love requires ongoing dedication and a willingness to adapt to each other's evolving needs and desires. This emphasizes the fragile nature of such a unique bond, highlighting the importance of nurturing it with thoughtful care and attention. Cultivating a healthy relationship demands not only passive affection but also an active commitment to understanding and supporting one another through life's challenges. In this next section, we'll explore how symbiosis and leadership shape the deep connections of romantic love and partnership, making them truly special.

2.3.1 Emotional Reciprocity and Safety

In terms of love, emotional reciprocity goes beyond mere fairness; it serves as a fundamental pillar for a thriving relationship. Each partner must feel free to openly share their innermost feelings, aspirations, uncertainties, and vulnerabilities without the looming threat of judgment or rejection. When approached with empathy and understanding, this type of sincere emotional exchange cultivates an environment of emotional safety. This safe space becomes fertile ground on which intimacy can flourish. When both partners actively engage in this process, they cultivate a deeper connection that strengthens their bond, fosters mutual trust, and establishes a solid foundation for a lasting partnership. In essence, emotional reciprocity is not merely a practice but a vital ingredient for a profound and enduring love.

☑ Leadership Parallel:

Leaders who cultivate psychological safety within their teams create a supportive environment where innovation flourishes and individuals feel empowered to be vulnerable. In such settings, team members are encouraged to share their ideas without fear of ridicule or backlash, fostering creativity and collaboration. Similarly, in personal relationships, emotional safety is crucial as it nurtures deep trust and allows individuals to reveal their true selves without reservation. This foundation of trust promotes open communication and a willingness to confront difficult emotions together.

Moreover, just as effective leaders prioritize active listening and empathy to ensure their team members feel heard and valued, caring partners in relationships adopt a similar approach. They focus on understanding their partner's feelings and perspectives rather than merely seeking to correct or fix them. This deep commitment to understanding fosters more meaningful connections and helps navigate challenges with compassion and patience. In both contexts, the presence of psychological and emotional safety is essential for nurturing growth, resilience, and authentic connections.

2.3.2 Shared Purpose and Vision

Symbiotic partnerships thrive when there is a shared sense of mission and purpose that transcends individual aspirations. While personal goals certainly hold significance, it is the alignment in core values, strategic direction, and envisioned legacy that truly cultivates long-term stability and success. When both parties are committed to a common objective, they can synergize their efforts, foster mutual growth, and overcome challenges together.

In contrast, without a unified vision, relationships can quickly lose their energy and focus. They may drift aimlessly, stagnate in growth, or even become emotionally unfulfilling. A lack of shared values and goals can result in misunderstandings and conflicts, gradually eroding the trust that binds them. Therefore, it is crucial to adopt a clear and inspiring vision to support deep, cooperative relationships capable of enduring and thriving amidst life's challenges.

☑ Leadership Parallel:

In the world of business, successful co-founders share a vision that serves as a guiding star for their endeavors. While each partner may bring unique strengths and talents to the table- one might be a visionary thinker and the other excels in operational efficiency- their collaborative spirit fosters an environment where innovation can thrive. Similarly, in the realm of love, couples who aspire together, meticulously craft plans for their future, and nurture each other's growth create a relationship that is not only resilient but also vibrant and continually transforming. This joint commitment transforms their bond into a rich tapestry of shared experiences, ambitions, and mutual support, laying the foundation for a lasting and harmonious partnership.

Relationship Example:

The relationship between Barack and Michelle Obama exemplifies a strong shared purpose and deep commitment. Throughout their journey, they have shown unwavering dedication to numerous community initiatives, from advocating for education reform and supporting veterans to tackling health disparities. Together, they have created a family that embodies their values of compassion and resilience, supporting their daughters while managing the challenges of public life. Their shared vision not only reinforces each other's individual goals but also enhances their collective influence on society. This partnership underscores the strength of collaboration in driving positive change, demonstrating how their united efforts extend well beyond their personal lives into the wider community.

2.3.3 Conflict Resolution and Accountability

Every loving relationship inevitably encounters conflict; this is a natural aspect of human interaction. However, what distinguishes symbiotic love from unstable romance is not the avoidance of disagreements but rather the presence of effective conflict resolution and mutual accountability. In a thriving relationship, partners approach their issues with grace and understanding. They engage in open communication, ensuring that both voices are heard and respected.

Grounded in humility, each partner recognizes their own flaws and is willing to accept responsibility for their part in any disagreement. They prioritize restoration and healing over the need to be right or win an argument. This focus on resolution fosters a deeper connection, allowing both individuals to grow together while reinforcing their bond. In essence, a healthy relationship thrives not on the absence of conflict but on the ability to navigate it constructively.

✅ Leadership Parallel:

Effective leaders skillfully navigate conflict by actively listening to all parties involved, taking responsibility for their actions, and focusing on shared objectives. Similarly, loving partners address conflicts together, collaborating rather than viewing each other as opponents. Their primary goal is to nurture harmony and understanding, valuing unity more than winning an argument.

2.3.4 Physical Intimacy as Mutual Giving

In romantic relationships, physical intimacy transcends mere physical connection; it embodies a profound act of vulnerability shared between partners. This intimate bond is not solely about the encounter itself but represents a mutual and sacrificial gift, encompassing both the joy of closeness and a deep awareness of each other's emotional and physical needs. Within the context of a committed partnership or marriage, intimacy serves as a foundational pillar that strengthens the relationship, acting as a bridge that fosters deeper understanding and connection.

Intimacy transcends love; it embodies a pact founded on trust, allowing both individuals to feel secure and motivated to express their authentic selves without judgment. This reciprocal sharing fosters a supportive and empathetic atmosphere, empowering partners to be present for each other during challenging moments, thus strengthening emotional safety and deepening their connection. Such a relationship instills a profound sense of belonging and acceptance, ensuring that each partner feels valued, appreciated, and understood.

As the relationship evolves, intimacy becomes a vital component, enriching the partnership and fostering resilience over time. It encourages open communication and shared experiences, which not only strengthen emotional ties but also promote personal growth. Ultimately, a healthy level of intimacy leads to a fulfilling relationship, where both partners thrive individually and together, navigating life's challenges as a united front.

☑ Leadership Parallel:

Great leaders inspire others by generously sharing from a place of abundance rather than from a sense of obligation. In nurturing relationships, the true essence of mutual giving within intimacy emerges from genuine affection and a sincere willingness to connect, not from a sense of duty or the subtle pressure of manipulation. When both partners in a relationship strive to give more than they receive, intimacy evolves into a beautifully symbiotic connection where love flourishes, allowing both individuals to grow together, deepening their bond and enriching their lives in profound ways.

2.3.5 Loyalty, Commitment, and Covenant

Symbiotic partnerships are formed not just on fleeting emotions but on a deep covenantal commitment that endures over time. This lasting promise transcends superficial attraction and possesses an inherent strength that enables it to face life's inevitable challenges, such as difficulties, changes, and personal growth. In these relationships, loyalty serves as the vital glue, uniting the partners even as the initial intensity of passion fades and life's complexities emerge.

Ultimately, this deep-seated loyalty fosters resilience, allowing individuals to navigate the ups and downs together and emerge stronger and more connected through shared experiences and unwavering support. Such partnerships thrive not only on love but also on a mutual commitment to nurturing each other's growth and well-being, making them richer and more fulfilling.

Ultimately, this deep-seated loyalty fosters resilience, allowing individuals to navigate the ups and downs together and emerge stronger and more connected through shared experiences and unwavering support. Through the highs and lows of shared experiences, they not only emerge stronger but also become deeply connected, united by the unwavering support they provide one another. Relationships like this flourish on a foundation of love and are enriched by a mutual commitment to nurturing each other's growth and well-being. This commitment enriches their relationship, turning each success and challenge into a foundation that fortifies their connection and adds to the beauty of their shared journey.

☑ **Leadership Parallel:**

Effective leadership grounded in a long-term commitment, rather than merely focusing on immediate outcomes, cultivates a profound and lasting impact within an organization. This approach highlights the importance of having a clear vision and a sense of stability, encouraging leaders to dedicate their time and resources toward building meaningful relationships and nurturing initiatives. These efforts may not yield quick results or instant gratification, but they establish a foundation for significant growth and transformation over time, ultimately shaping a resilient and flourishing community.

In romantic relationships, a strong commitment nurtures resilience and mutual understanding. It creates a space where partners can navigate the inevitable highs and lows of their shared journey. This deep commitment supports key elements such as perseverance, which helps couples overcome challenges; forgiveness, which facilitates healing from conflicts; and trust, which strengthens their bond during difficult times. Ultimately, this robust foundation ensures that a relationship not only survives but also thrives in the face of life's changes.

2.3.6 Recognizing and Healing Unhealthy Attachments

Not every romantic relationship fosters mutual growth and support; some can become harmful and unequal. When one partner consistently takes control, manipulates, or emotionally drains the other, the relationship shifts from a healthy connection to a parasitic one. In these cases, the needs of one individual overshadow those of the other, leading to a toxic dynamic that can adversely affect both partners.

It's crucial to recognize signs of toxicity to address these harmful patterns. Common indicators include codependency, where one partner heavily relies on the other for emotional support; control, in which one partner governs the terms of the relationship; and avoidance, where one or both partners avoid discussing issues, leading to unresolved conflicts. Identifying these behaviors represents the first step toward healing- whether that involves collaborating to repair the relationship or making the difficult choice to separate for personal well-being. Valuing emotional health and fostering authentic connections are essential components in nurturing satisfying romantic relationships.

Leadership Application:

Leaders bear the critical responsibility of fostering a healthy environment for their teams by actively identifying and eliminating toxic behaviors. This not only protects the mental and emotional well-being of team members but also enhances overall productivity and morale. Similarly, individuals in various types of relationships must prioritize their emotional and spiritual health by establishing clear boundaries and recognizing their own needs.

Using tools like counseling can offer valuable guidance and support in navigating complex emotions and conflicts. Accountability, whether through trusted friends or professional assistance, serves as a vital mechanism for maintaining one's well-being and ensuring that relationships stay healthy and nurturing. Ultimately, if a relationship consistently undermines one's sense of self-worth or happiness, it may be necessary to consider walking away, thereby preserving personal integrity and fostering a more balanced life.

Chapter 2.3 Summary: Love/Partnerships: Building Covenant through Symbiosis

Romantic relationships thrive on reciprocity, emotional safety, and shared purpose.

- Romantic relationships thrive when partners mutually exchange affection and support, fostering emotional safety where both feel valued and understood. This nurturing environment promotes vulnerability and trust, allowing individuals to share their innermost thoughts and feelings without fear of judgment. Furthermore, a shared purpose, whether common goals, dreams, or values, reinforces the bond, enabling couples to navigate challenges together and celebrate their journey as a united team.

Conflict is not the enemy; disconnection is. Healing comes through humility and accountability.

- Conflict isn't the true adversary; the disconnection between individuals poses the real threat. True healing emerges from a place of humility, where we acknowledge our imperfections, and from a commitment to accountability, where we take responsibility for our actions and their impact on others. Embracing these principles cultivates a deeper connection and paves the way for meaningful resolutions.

Intimacy, loyalty, and love that lasts beyond emotion.

- When intimacy, unwavering loyalty, and trust come together, they create a foundation for a love that goes beyond just passing feelings. This deep connection builds a lasting bond that can weather any storm, nurtures trust, and creates a warm, safe space for growth and understanding.

Leadership in love means servant-hearted pursuit, mutual growth, and courageous vulnerability.

- Leadership rooted in love embodies a servant-hearted pursuit, prioritizing the needs and aspirations of others. This approach fosters an environment of mutual growth, encouraging individuals to flourish together by sharing knowledge and experiences that enrich each other's journeys. Furthermore, it requires courageous vulnerability as leaders open their hearts to share their struggles and strengths, thus building a foundation of trust and authenticity that inspires others to do the same.

🔑 Leadership Takeaway:

To truly love is to lead with a deep sense of empathy, unwavering commitment, profound humility, and a clear sense of purpose. Symbiotic relationships are not mere happenstance; they are nurtured and cultivated through intentional investments of time and energy, shared spiritual alignment, and a foundation of emotional honesty. These connections thrive when we actively engage with one another, fostering an environment where both individuals can grow and flourish together.

2.4 Co-workers: Collaborating Through Symbiotic Leadership™

Workplaces function as vital ecosystems where individuals from various cultural backgrounds and different personalities unite to achieve common goals. However, the relationships that form within these environments are often confined to transactional exchanges, significantly influenced by existing hierarchies, relentless deadlines, and competitive pressures. Consequently, many employees may find themselves assigned to positions that emphasize compliance and efficiency rather than genuine connections and meaningful collaboration. This situation can hinder creativity and limit the ability to foster a supportive and inclusive workplace culture.

In contrast, the concept of symbiosis in the workplace provides a more enriching alternative. This model cultivates an environment where coworkers can thrive by actively supporting one another, sharing knowledge, and fostering mutual respect. In a symbiotic workplace, collaboration becomes the norm rather than the exception, promoting open communication and creative problem-solving. By valuing each person's unique contributions and perspectives, this approach not only enhances job satisfaction but also drives innovation and productivity. Ultimately, a symbiotic relationship among colleagues transforms mere coexistence into a vibrant community where everyone succeeds together.

2.4.1 Mutual Contribution in Team Environments

Members of a healthy and effective team share their distinct expertise, insights, and energy, collaborating toward a common goal. This interaction parallels the concept of symbiosis found in nature, where diverse organisms flourish by utilizing one another's strengths to create a harmonious ecosystem. When individuals are encouraged to work within their unique skill sets while showing respect and appreciation for each other's contributions, the entire team enjoys substantial benefits.

This collaborative environment not only boosts productivity but also improves overall morale. When team members feel valued and engaged, they are more likely to be motivated to share ideas, take the initiative, and contribute to discussions. This openness promotes enhanced creativity and innovative problem-solving, allowing the team to address challenges from various perspectives. Furthermore, the sense of community that develops within the team encourages stronger interpersonal relationships and trust among members. By celebrating each other's successes and supporting one another through challenges, the team fosters a culture of continuous improvement and adaptability.

In the end, this collaboration turns challenges into chances for growth, allowing the team to tackle complexities with flexibility and strength. This leads to a fruitful success cycle that not only meets objectives but also promotes the professional growth and personal satisfaction of each member. Such a comprehensive teamwork strategy not only delivers results but also fosters a rewarding and sustainable workplace.

Leadership Parallel:

Effective leaders understand that micromanagement hinders creativity and harms team morale. Instead, they take on the role of facilitators, striving to foster an environment where synergy can thrive. By recognizing and appreciating the unique strengths of each team member, these leaders encourage collaboration and leverage the various skills within their team.

They emphasize open communication and mutual respect, making sure everyone feels acknowledged and valued. In this way, they not only remove obstacles that could impede progress but also nurture a culture of trust and support.

This concept of Symbiotic Leadership™ transcends simple tolerance of differences; it actively celebrates each individual's unique perspectives and backgrounds, harnessing these differences to foster innovation and problem-solving. Ultimately, effective leaders unite their teams around a shared vision, cultivating a sense of belonging and collective purpose that empowers everyone to succeed together.

Corporate Example:

Cross-functional teams at companies like Pixar and IDEO exemplify the power of leveraging diverse perspectives and expertise. These teams unite individuals with various backgrounds, including creative visionaries, technical specialists, and strategic thinkers, who collaborate in environments founded on mutual respect and cooperation. This vibrant blend of ideas cultivates an environment that is advantageous to innovation. Rather than competing against one another, team members share insights and expertise, fostering the emergence of collective brilliance. This collaboration not only enhances creativity but also leads to unique solutions that might not arise in a less diverse environment. By valuing each member's contributions, organizations cultivate a dynamic atmosphere where collaboration fuels innovation.

2.4.2 Communication and Psychological Safety

Workplace relationships frequently suffer in the absence of open, honest, and respectful communication. This vital component nurtures an environment where psychological safety flourishes, allowing individuals to express their thoughts, concerns, or even mistakes without fear of embarrassment or retaliation. Such a setting is crucial for building trust among colleagues, as it promotes vulnerability and nurtures stronger connections.

In symbiotic work relationships, team members collaborate effectively and foster a culture where everyone is acknowledged, listened to, and appreciated. This mutual recognition boosts engagement and productivity, empowering individuals to contribute their best selves to the team. When employees feel respected and valued for their contributions, it enhances morale and strengthens their commitment to shared goals. By emphasizing open communication and psychological safety, organizations can cultivate healthier, more effective workplace relationships that ultimately contribute to success.

☑ **Leadership Parallel:**

Leaders practicing empathetic communication and attentive listening foster an environment that nurtures innovative ideas. By emphasizing transparency and welcoming feedback, these leaders establish a culture of open dialogue, encouraging team members to express their thoughts and perspectives freely. This reciprocal approach encourages a culture rooted in trust and collaboration, which enhances a workplace that prioritizes relational well-being. In this environment, employees experience respect and appreciation, fostering increased creativity, improved morale, and a deeper sense of community within the organization. When leaders show a sincere commitment to understanding and valuing diverse perspectives, they nurture a dynamic ecosystem of ideas and solutions.

2.4.3 Accountability and Integrity in Professional Relationships

Trust within a team is built through a combination of consistent commitment, respect for deadlines, and mutual acknowledgment of responsibilities for both successes and setbacks. It is crucial for team members to exhibit reliability through their actions; meeting deadlines and fulfilling obligations not only demonstrates dedication but also fosters confidence in each other's abilities. Such trust serves as a foundation for effective collaboration, flourishing in a workplace culture that actively encourages both accountability and compassion, allowing individuals to feel valued and respected as they work toward shared goals.

In this nurturing environment, when mistakes inevitably occur, which they do in any dynamic team, they are not viewed as failures to be punished but as valuable opportunities for collective learning and growth. This shift in perspective transforms what could be a discouraging situation into a chance for constructive dialogue and improvement of team processes. Team members are encouraged to collaboratively analyze what went wrong, understand the underlying issues, and devise strategies to prevent similar occurrences in the future, thus turning errors into teachable moments that contribute to the team's overall resilience and effectiveness.

Effective communication is essential in this setting. Team members need to feel secure in acknowledging their errors without fearing consequences, fostering a trust-based culture that prioritizes honesty over perfection. This transparency encourages more active collaboration, enabling individuals to help each other tackle challenges and seek help when needed. When team members are at ease sharing their opinions and worries, it results in more innovative solutions and nurtures a sense of belonging within the group, ultimately boosting overall performance.

Celebrating successes is equally important and should be a team effort rather than a solitary activity. Acknowledging achievements collectively reinforces the team's unity and fosters a sense of shared accomplishment, making each member feel like an essential part of the success. This practice not only boosts morale but also emphasizes that everyone's contributions matter, creating an inclusive atmosphere where individuals are motivated to continue supporting one another. By sharing celebrations, teams cultivate a spirit of solidarity, which further enhances their collaborative efforts and drives ongoing success.

In summary, by creating a culture that balances accountability with kindness, our teams can significantly enhance their overall effectiveness. This approach entails clear communication of expectations and responsibilities while nurturing an environment of compassion and understanding. This dual focus not only strengthens interpersonal relationships but also fosters a resilient team that can navigate challenges and celebrate triumphs together, ultimately driving collective success.

Leadership Parallel:

Accountability must be embraced at every level of an organization, fostering a culture of collective responsibility instead of just flowing from the top. Effective leaders demonstrate genuine accountability by honestly recognizing their mistakes, thus providing a strong example for their teams. They celebrate the achievements of others, highlighting contributions that might otherwise go unnoticed. By welcoming and promoting constructive feedback, they foster an environment that values open dialogue, enabling team members to express their opinions confidently. This approach nurtures mutual integrity, reinforcing team bonds and encouraging a collaborative environment where everyone is engaged in one another's success.

Corporate Example:

Companies that embody strong organizational values, like Chick-fil-A, often experience significantly higher employee retention and morale. This effect cannot be attributed solely to competitive pay; rather, it arises from a culture that prioritizes respect, exceptional service, and a collective sense of responsibility among team members. Employees are valued not only for their skills and expertise but also for their role in creating a positive and collaborative work environment. Such an environment builds loyalty and motivates individuals to cherish their roles, resulting in higher job satisfaction and enhanced company performance.

2.4.4 Navigating Competition and Collaboration

Healthy ambition can significantly enhance both individual and team performance, motivating everyone to achieve their potential. However, when competition among coworkers becomes excessive, it can create toxic environments that undermine collaboration and hinder overall effectiveness. In a genuinely collaborative team environment, collaboration is not merely encouraged; it becomes the standard practice for the group.

In these environments, team members begin to view one another not as competitors vying for recognition or resources but as essential partners united by a common goal. This change in viewpoint cultivates a climate of trust and transparency, enabling individuals to share their thoughts and opinions openly without worrying about criticism or negative consequences. When team members feel secure in their roles, it develops a sense of belonging, where each individual feels valued and empowered to share their unique strengths and perspectives.

A collaborative environment fosters innovation by uniting diverse ideas to solve problems creatively. When team members prioritize common goals over individual accolades, they can effectively leverage their collective strengths, leading to more significant and impactful results for the group.

Ultimately, when team members engage in a collaborative pursuit of shared goals, they not only achieve significant outcomes but also foster a vibrant and positive workplace culture that enhances job satisfaction and supports ongoing personal and professional growth. In this environment, success is measured not just by individual accomplishments but by the shared victories that strengthen team cohesion and promote sustainable progress.

✅ Leadership Parallel:

Effective leaders prioritize the team's accomplishments over personal aspirations, advancing a collaborative and cohesive atmosphere. They actively cultivate a culture that values collective objectives and shared successes, encouraging team members to support one another in achieving these goals. By fostering an environment that acknowledges contributions as a collective effort, leaders reduce the temptation for individualistic successes and self-centered actions.

This method not only strengthens team unity but also improves overall performance, as individuals develop a stronger sense of accountability and a shared motivation to strive towards common goals. As a result, the emphasis is on effectively leveraging each member's strengths to benefit the team, leading to lasting success and a more fulfilling workplace for everyone involved. In this supportive atmosphere, isolated efforts and self-serving behaviors are actively discouraged as they can undermine teamwork and lower morale. Instead, leaders promote open communication and cooperation, enabling team members to leverage each other's strengths and work collaboratively towards achieving their objectives. This approach enhances overall performance and cultivates a sense of belonging and camaraderie among team members, ultimately leading to a more cohesive and effective unit.

2.4.5 Conflict and Restoration in the Workplace

Disagreements are a natural part of professional environments, arising from individuals' various perspectives and experiences. While these differences can create tension, our conflict resolution approach is crucial. How we handle disagreements ultimately shapes the quality of our workplace relationships and influences our organizational culture.

In a thriving workplace, coworkers engage in symbiotic relationships, understanding the importance of addressing issues directly while maintaining mutual respect and empathy. They recognize that open communication is essential; it enables individuals to express their thoughts and feelings freely, ensuring that everyone feels heard, acknowledged, and valued. This inclusivity fosters a safe space for dialogue and helps to prevent misunderstandings from escalating into larger disputes.

Instead of letting unresolved conflicts linger and create resentment within the team, these individuals promote collaborative problem-solving strategies. They aim to identify solutions that are both just and beneficial for everyone involved. This teamwork-centered method can manifest in different ways, including brainstorming sessions, mediation, or casual discussions that foster creative thinking and compromise.

By actively fostering an environment where differing opinions are expressed constructively, coworkers can transform potential discord into valuable opportunities for growth, innovation, and stronger partnerships. This approach enriches team dynamics, enhances overall productivity, and cultivates a culture of trust and collaboration, ultimately benefiting the entire organization. In this manner, conflicts become not just challenges to overcome but catalysts for deeper understanding and improved teamwork.

☑ Leadership Parallel:

Healthy leaders significantly influence their teams' culture by setting explicit norms for conflict resolution. They tackle disagreements with honesty, professionalism, and a commitment to reconciliation. Effective leaders ensure fairness in mediating disputes, making certain that all individuals feel heard and appreciated. They practice active listening to uncover underlying concerns and emotions, which enhances understanding among team members. Even during conflicts, they maintain dignity and respect, promoting open communication and collaborative solutions. By exemplifying these behaviors, leaders not only resolve conflicts but also foster a more resilient and unified team environment.

Case Example:

In numerous agile organizations, practices such as retrospectives play a crucial role in creating safe spaces where team members can openly reflect on past projects and performance. These sessions offer an opportunity to celebrate successes and analyze areas that need improvement. Creating a trusting environment allows individuals to freely express their thoughts and experiences, without the risk of judgment. This organized method promotes open communication while also functioning as a restorative means for resolving conflicts. It motivates participants to collaboratively and constructively tackle challenges, resulting in more effective problem-solving and enhanced team dynamics in the future.

2.4.6 Recognizing and Addressing Toxic Coworker Relationships

While workplace relationships can often be positive and collaborative, not all of them contribute to a healthy work environment. In many instances, destructive behaviors such as gossip, sabotage, and passive-aggressive interactions can profoundly undermine team cohesion. These toxic dynamics create an atmosphere where trust erodes, leaving team members reluctant to engage openly or share ideas. As trust diminishes, communication becomes strained, and collaboration falters, stifling creativity and innovation.

Furthermore, a lack of accountability among team members can intensify tensions. When individuals neglect to own their actions or fulfill their commitments, it can lead to overlooked tasks, creating confusion and frustration. This absence of personal accountability may foster a culture of blame-shifting, where team members prioritize their positions over mutual support. When parasitic behaviors arise, they deplete morale and productivity. Employees might experience heightened stress and disengagement, resulting in increased turnover and a loss of institutional knowledge. This disengagement can gradually spread through the organization, affecting both individual performance and the team's overall success. A toxic work environment discourages collaboration, stifles growth, and undermines the organization's shared goals, underscoring the importance of nurturing healthy workplace relationships.

✅ Leadership Application:

Leaders bear a vital duty to promptly and transparently tackle toxicity within their teams. By swiftly addressing issues, they contribute to a safe and positive workplace that reflects the organization's core values. This entails encouraging open communication, attentively listening to concerns, and decisively acting to resolve conflicts before they worsen.

In addition to the role of leadership, individual team members also play a crucial part in maintaining a healthy atmosphere. They should be encouraged to set personal boundaries to protect their emotional well-being. This involves recognizing signs of stress or discomfort and proactively seeking resolutions, whether through direct conversations, mediation, or shifting focus. By prioritizing both leadership accountability and individual responsibility, teams can cultivate a culture of respect, support, and mutual accountability.

Chapter 2.4 Summary: Coworkers Collaborating Through Symbiotic Leadership™

Workplace symbiosis flourishes through shared goals, mutual respect, and psychological safety.

- Workplace symbiosis flourishes when team members come together to pursue common goals, creating an atmosphere where mutual respect is fundamental to collaboration. This cooperation is further bolstered by psychological safety, which encourages individuals to share their thoughts and ideas without the fear of being judged. When employees perceive themselves as valued and safe, they are more inclined to take initiative, propose innovative solutions, and tackle challenges as a team. Consequently, organizations can develop a dynamic and resilient workforce that not only achieves objectives but also adapts and grows collectively in response to changing demands.

Effective communication, accountability, and humility are essential for a productive team environment.

- Clear and open communication, a strong sense of accountability, and a spirit of humility are fundamental elements that foster a thriving team environment. When team members engage in effective communication, they freely share ideas and feedback, creating a culture of trust and collaboration. Accountability ensures that individuals take responsibility for their actions and commitments, enhancing reliability and strengthening team dynamics. Additionally, humility allows team members to value each other's contributions, encouraging a supportive atmosphere where everyone feels respected and heard. Together, these elements not only enhance teamwork but also drive the overall success of the organization.

Healthy conflict resolution and value alignment enhance trust and performance.

- Effectively navigating conflicts and aligning core values fosters a deep sense of trust, significantly boosting overall performance within a team or organization. When individuals engage in healthy conflict resolution, they not only address disagreements constructively but also establish a framework for open communication and mutual respect. This intentional approach strengthens relationships, creates a positive work environment, and enhances collaborative efforts, ultimately leading to improved outcomes and shared success.

Address toxic behaviors with clear communication, strong leadership, and courage.

- Address toxic behaviors by demonstrating open communication, showcasing strong leadership, and displaying consistent courage. It is essential to create an environment where individuals can freely express their concerns and where leaders exhibit integrity and resilience in the face of challenges. This proactive approach not only addresses negative behaviors but also advances a culture grounded in respect and accountability.

🔑 **Leadership Takeaway:**

Building co-worker relationships, similar to creating effective teams, requires intentional effort, emotional intelligence, and collective commitment. Both leaders and team members influence the culture with their words, actions, and readiness to support one another. When workplace relationships evolve into a symbiotic nature, organizations not only advance but truly thrive.

2.5 Mentorship/Coaching: Symbiosis Through Guidance

Mentorship and coaching demonstrate a unique and intentional symbiotic relationship characterized by a vibrant exchange of knowledge and support. In this relationship, the mentor or coach shares extensive wisdom, life experiences, and motivational encouragement, offering guidance based on lessons drawn from both triumphs and setbacks. Meanwhile, the mentee or pupil brings a desire to learn, a fresh perspective, and a reservoir of untapped potential.

Although these roles might seem uneven at first, with the mentor holding more knowledge, successful mentorships typically transform into cooperative partnerships. Throughout this process, both individuals participate in a collaboration where the mentor learns from the mentee's distinct perspectives and experiences. This mutual exchange creates a space of joint investment, enabling both participants to evolve and enhance their development not only in their respective roles but also as individuals.

With open communication and a shared commitment to growth, mentorship relationships can evolve into strong partnerships that provide personal and professional enrichment for both the mentor and mentee. This journey fosters co-creation, allowing them to face challenges together and celebrate their successes, ultimately strengthening their bond and boosting their skills.

2.5.1 The Symbiotic Flow of Knowledge and Growth

In a nurturing mentorship or coaching relationship, both parties experience wonderful growth that is vibrant and enriching. The mentor is essential in offering guidance, sharing expertise, and delivering insightful feedback drawn from personal experiences. Yet, the relationship isn't just about the mentor; the mentee injects new energy, innovative ideas, and distinct viewpoints that enhance the interaction's engagement and relevance.

This reciprocal exchange creates a powerful learning environment where both parties benefit, not only in skills and knowledge but also personally. The mentor gains new insights and a renewed sense of purpose through their interactions, while the mentee develops confidence and a clearer sense of direction in their personal and professional journey. Ultimately, this cyclical relationship fosters an enriching experience that enhances the capabilities and growth of both individuals involved.

Leadership Parallel:

Exceptional leaders embody the roles of both teachers and learners. They prioritize continuous education, showing a deep commitment to their personal and professional growth. They create a culture of open communication and trust by welcoming various perspectives. This willingness to listen enriches their understanding and enhances innovation within their teams. Furthermore, they skillfully adjust their guidance and strategies, taking real-time feedback into account to ensure their advice stays relevant and impactful. In doing so, they motivate those around them to pursue excellence and embrace growth.

2.5.2 Trust and Accountability in Mentorship

Trust serves as a reciprocal exchange in mentorship relationships. It establishes a foundation for open discussions and authentic feedback, essential for personal and professional growth. Lacking this trust significantly reduces the potential for meaningful reflection, hindering mentees' ability to accept constructive criticism.

In the same way, when accountability is integrated into these relationships, it transforms from merely a corrective measure into a strong and supportive process that's centered on growth and development. This shift creates a more supportive environment where individuals feel encouraged to take risks, learn from their mistakes, and grow. In this setting, mentors can provide insights and guidance that not only address shortcomings but also cultivate strengths, fostering a culture of continuous improvement and mutual respect.

☑ **Leadership Parallel:**

Mentors and coaches act as accountability partners, helping individuals stay true to their goals while demonstrating unwavering personal integrity. They offer constructive feedback with a compassionate approach, nurturing an environment that promotes growth. Their inspiring belief instills a sense of purpose in others, motivating them to overcome challenges and stay committed to their aspirations.

2.5.3 Coaching for Alignment and Confidence

Coaching, whether in athletics, the corporate sector, or personal development, plays a crucial role in helping individuals align their inherent talents with their aspirations and goals. A skilled coach does not create talent; rather, they act as a catalyst, drawing out and enhancing the potential that already exists within a person. This process involves nurturing a deep sense of clarity, enabling individuals to understand their strengths and weaknesses, and instilling the confidence necessary to take actionable steps toward achieving their objectives. A skilled coach provides personalized guidance, continuous support, and helpful feedback, empowering individuals to overcome obstacles, enhance their abilities, and achieve greater success in their personal and professional lives.

Leadership Parallel:

Great coaches empower others by asking questions instead of giving commands. They elevate those around them by identifying blind spots and promoting self-awareness. They skillfully enhance individuals' capabilities by identifying overlooked growth areas and promoting a deep sense of self-awareness. By asking insightful and reflective questions, these coaches adeptly help individuals reveal their hidden strengths and explore new paths for growth, fostering a journey of both personal and professional change.

Chapter 2.5 Summary: Mentorship/Coaching - Symbiosis Through Guidance

Mentoring and coaching relationships benefit both the teacher and the learner.

- Mentoring and coaching relationships create a vibrant growth environment for both teachers and learners. Through these interactions, teachers gain valuable insights and new perspectives, enhancing their skills and methods. At the same time, learners receive tailored guidance and support that promotes their development and builds their confidence. This exchange enriches understanding and fosters a collaborative atmosphere where both individuals can flourish and grow together.

Trust, respect, and accountability form the bedrock of transformation.

- The foundation of meaningful transformation rests on the pillars of trust, respect, and accountability. Trust nurtures open communication and strengthens relationships, while respect recognizes the inherent worth of every individual involved in the process. Accountability guarantees that commitments are fulfilled and responsibilities recognized, creating a space where individuals feel empowered to engage and develop. These components together nurture a dynamic environment that promotes enduring change.

Symbiosis in guidance relationships is about serving one another's future with intentionality and grace.

- Symbiosis in guidance relationships highlights the shared commitment to thoughtfully and elegantly nurture each other's futures. It requires a profound understanding of each other's aspirations and challenges, creating a space where both parties can flourish together. Through intentional actions, individuals in these relationships not only uplift each other's journeys but also establish a harmonious balance of reciprocity characterized by kindness and respect.

2.6 Daily Interactions: Practicing Micro-Symbiosis

Not every symbiotic relationship is defined by long-term commitment or profound emotional ties. In fact, some of the most impactful relational moments occur during our daily encounters, often in settings we might deem mundane. Consider the brief interactions with baristas who craft our morning coffee, ride-share drivers who navigate us through bustling city streets, or the cashiers who scan our groceries with a friendly smile. Even exchanges with neighbors or colleagues we pass in the hallway can possess significant potential.

These micro-moments serve as unique opportunities to cultivate relational value. A simple gesture, such as a warm greeting or a genuine compliment, can brighten someone's day and foster a sense of connection. By taking a moment to acknowledge another person's presence, we sow seeds of encouragement, dignity, and kindness that resonate well beyond the fleeting interaction. These small acts of humanity, though often overlooked, possess the power to create ripples that enhance our communities and enrich our lives.

2.6.1 Choosing Respect in Every Encounter

Respect should extend beyond our close relationships. It is a critical mindset that should influence every interaction, no matter how brief it is. In a world that feels increasingly disconnected and isolated, even small gestures such as showing empathy, exercising patience, and being genuinely attentive can have a profound impact on our connections. These subtle acts can bridge gaps between individuals, foster a sense of community, and emphasize our shared humanity. By promoting a culture of respect in every interaction, we help build a more compassionate and interconnected world.

☑ Leadership Parallel:

Leaders are characterized not only by their relationships with top executives but also by their engagement with every team member in the organization, including those in less visible roles like janitors. This highlights the significance of appreciating all contributions. These everyday interactions serve as a true reflection of a leader's core values and principles. Symbiotic leaders possess the unique ability to make others feel recognized and valued, regardless of their position. Even a simple interaction, such as a friendly greeting, a sincere smile, or a brief moment of eye contact, can express respect and recognition. By doing so, leaders cultivate an inclusive culture where every team member feels recognized and valued, which enhances teamwork and motivation in the work environment. Even minor interactions can greatly influence team morale and effectiveness.

2.6.2 Daily Kindness as Cultural Currency

The way we engage in small interactions plays a crucial role in shaping the culture that surrounds us. Simple gestures, such as offering a genuine compliment, sharing a warm smile, or expressing gratitude with a heartfelt "thank you," may seem trivial at first glance. However, these seemingly minor acts convey a deeper sense of respect and appreciation. They have the ability to elevate the spirits of people around us, creating a setting in which individuals feel recognized and appreciated. By nurturing this positive environment through small yet impactful interactions, we not only enhance our own lives but also help build a shared culture of kindness and inclusivity where everyone feels inspired to connect and flourish.

Corporate Example:

Chick-fil-A has cultivated a distinctive culture centered around respect and exceptional service, encapsulated by the courteous phrase "my pleasure." This commitment to kindness in everyday interactions not only enhances the customer experience but also defines the brand itself. By prioritizing genuine hospitality and advancing a positive atmosphere, Chick-fil-A demonstrates that small gestures of kindness can significantly shape the values and overall identity of an organization. This culture of respect resonates not only with customers but also empowers employees, creating a unified and uplifting environment that sets the company apart in the highly competitive restaurant industry.

2.6.3 Micro-Symbiosis in a Digital World

Each interaction we engage in, whether it's through texts, emails, or social media comments, presents unique opportunities for micro-symbiosis, small-scale mutual support that can strengthen our connections with others. The tone we use, the speed of our responses, and the thoughtfulness we demonstrate can greatly impact the emotional state of those receiving our messages. A warm, supportive message can uplift someone's spirits, fostering a sense of connection and positivity. Conversely, a hasty or dismissive reply may leave others feeling ignored or deflated. By being mindful of our digital interactions, we can cultivate a more empathetic and positive online environment that not only strengthens our relationships but also encourages a culture of kindness and understanding.

☑ **Leadership Parallel:**

Leaders play a pivotal role in shaping the atmosphere of digital communication. Their actions, whether recognizing and valuing contributions in a lively group chat or responding with understanding and humility during moments of miscommunication, create a foundation of trust and reinforce relational equity. These seemingly minor yet impactful choices nurture a culture of openness and collaboration, fostering deeper connections among team members and enhancing overall engagement in a virtual environment.

For example, a leader who acknowledges and praises team members for their creative ideas not only boosts morale but also fosters a culture of active involvement and innovative thinking. When individuals feel recognized for their contributions, it sparks enthusiasm, motivating them to share their ideas more openly. Conversely, a leader who calmly addresses misunderstandings using effective communication skills can successfully diffuse potential tension. This thoughtful approach nurtures an environment where team members feel valued and secure, motivating them to express their thoughts and concerns openly.

These seemingly minor yet significant choices greatly nurture a culture of openness and collaboration. By modeling effective communication practices, leaders cultivate opportunities for stronger connections among team members. This, in turn, boosts overall engagement in a virtual setting, ensuring that team members are not merely participants but also active contributors to a shared mission. Ultimately, a leader's style establishes the tone for interactions, guiding the team toward a more cohesive and productive digital workspace.

Chapter 2.6 Summary: Daily Interactions - Practicing Micro-Symbiosis

Every interaction presents an opportunity to enhance relational dignity.

- Each interaction offers a precious opportunity to elevate and respect the intrinsic dignity of our relationships. By fostering a deeper sense of respect and connection among individuals, we can create an atmosphere that nurtures genuine understanding and compassion. These moments serve as building blocks for stronger bonds and a more harmonious community.

Daily habits of kindness, gratitude, and listening can create ripples, influencing the emotional tone of homes, workplaces, and communities.

- Engaging in daily practices of kindness, gratitude, and active listening can create powerful ripples that profoundly impact the emotional atmosphere of our homes, workplaces, and communities. These small yet significant actions cultivate a culture of compassion and positivity, fostering a nurturing environment where relationships thrive and individuals feel valued and heard. By consistently choosing to express kindness, recognize the good around us, and genuinely listen to others, we can transform our surroundings into havens of support and understanding, ultimately enriching the lives of everyone involved.

True leadership is demonstrated in the little things, not just the big decisions.

- True leadership is shown in major choices and the small, daily actions that influence a team's culture and morale. It exists in considerate gestures, supportive words, and a focus on individual needs that build trust and create a sense of belonging.

Chapter 2 Summary: The Different Types of Relationships

Relationships provide the context in which human potential can be cultivated or constrained. This chapter explores how symbiosis, the principle of mutual benefit, interdependence, and growth applies across six distinct types of relationships, offering insights into enhancing each form through intentional investment, trust, and alignment with biblical and leadership principles.

From family to the workplace, from lifelong friendships to brief daily encounters, every type of relationship, regardless of size, offers the chance to either contribute to or hinder the growth and well-being of others. In healthy relationships, we learn to give and receive, challenge and encourage, lead and serve. These interactions not only empower individuals but also foster enduring, resilient, and purposeful relationships.

🔑 Key Takeaways from Each Relationship Type:

2.1 Family – The First Environment for Symbiosis

The family is the first training ground for emotional intelligence, respect, and shared responsibility. This symbiosis is cultivated through mutual support, forgiveness, and accountability, establishing a solid foundation for all future relationships.

2.2 Friends – A Chosen Symbiotic Relationship

Friendship flourishes when both individuals engage emotionally, challenge one another with love, and maintain loyalty throughout different times. These selected bonds exemplify the strength found in safe vulnerability and mutual support.

2.3 Love/Partnerships – Building Covenant Through Symbiosis

Romantic relationships demand a covenant of commitment, emotional security, and a co-created vision. In this sense, true love is not a passive experience; it is actively nurtured through mutual engagement, accountability, and loyalty.

2.4 Co-workers – Collaborating Through Symbiotic Leadership™

Workplace relationships thrive in cultures of collaboration, clear communication, and shared success. Leaders and teams must prioritize respect, psychological safety, and fairness to sustain professional symbiosis.

2.5 Mentorship and Coaching – Symbiosis Through Guidance

Mentoring and coaching relationships thrive on humility, trust, and mutual growth. When mentors act with the heart of a teacher and mentees respond with a willingness to learn, both undergo transformation.

2.6 Daily Interactions – Practicing Micro-Symbiosis

Even the briefest encounters can embody the essence of symbiosis. Daily respect, kindness, and attentiveness ripple outward, shaping culture and reflecting the universe's fractal image in the ordinary moments of life.

🔄 Unifying Themes of Symbiotic Relationships:

Across every type of relationship explored in this chapter, five consistent patterns emerge:

1. **Mutual Investment** – Thriving relationships are not one-sided; they grow through reciprocal contribution.
2. **Accountability With Grace** – Healthy dynamics embrace responsibility while extending forgiveness.

3. **Shared Purpose** – Whether explicit or implied, relationships are strengthened by alignment in values and vision.

4. **Emotional Safety and Trust** – Vulnerability is the soil in which intimacy and collaboration grow.

5. **Intentionality and Leadership** – Strong relationships don't happen accidentally; they are led with intention and love.

Looking Ahead: Leadership Theories Reimagined

Now that we've explored how symbiosis occurs in every relationship, we will focus on the leadership theories that explain how individuals grow, perform, and interact in structured environments. In Chapter 3, we will analyze classic leadership frameworks, including Maslow's Hierarchy, McGregor's X and Y Theory, McClelland's Needs Theory, and others, and begin examining how Symbiotic Relationship Theory™ (SRT) contributes uniquely to this evolving conversation.

CHAPTER 3
REIMAGINING LEADERSHIP
THROUGH SYMBIOSIS

Chapter 3: Reimagining Leadership Through Symbiosis

Leadership theories have long sought to define how individuals develop, what motivates them, and how organizations should operate. From Maslow's Hierarchy of Needs to McGregor's Theory X and Theory Y, these frameworks have influenced generations of leaders, educators, and thinkers. However, as powerful as these models are, many fail in one crucial aspect: they often separate individual achievement from relational context.

The reality is that no one grows in a vacuum. No family thrives in isolation. No team succeeds without trust. Relationships, whether interdependent, evolving, and adaptive, form the true ecosystem where leadership, growth, and transformation occur. This truth requires a fresh perspective on leadership. One that considers not just individuals but also the spaces between them. It evaluates not only personal ambition and behavioral tendencies but also the quality of connections that enable communities to thrive.

I refer to that lens as the **Symbiotic Relationship Theory™ (SRT)**.

This theory suggests that the most sustainable and transformative relationships- be they personal or professional- are characterized by mutual investment, a shared purpose, emotional safety, and reciprocal accountability. Unlike traditional theories that emphasize individual motivation or hierarchical control, SRT focuses on **Intentional Interdependence**.

SRT asks not just *how do you grow,* but *how do we grow together?*

This theory is not confined to just one area of life. Whether it pertains to family, friendship, mentorship, or marriage, SRT provides a comprehensive approach to relational health. However, it has become particularly potent in the fields of leadership and organizational culture, which is why it has led to the development of an applied model: the **Symbiotic Workplace Model™ (SWM).**

The Symbiotic Workplace Model™ (SWM) introduces the principles of Symbiotic Relationship Theory™ (SRT) within organizations. It shifts workplaces from environments focused on compliance and control to ecosystems characterized by shared responsibility, empowerment, and growth. Leaders transition from enforcers to facilitators, while teams evolve into interconnected units fostering creative exchange. Feedback circulates in all directions. Accountability is complemented by grace. Culture is integrated into strategy.

This chapter will explore how *Symbiotic Relationship Theory™* and the *Symbiotic Workplace Model™* not only align with but also enhance the most recognized leadership theories in modern history. You'll see how:

- Maslow's focus on individual needs is expanded into mutual needs.
- McGregor's assumptions about motivation are reframed through shared trust and accountability.
- McClelland's needs for achievement and affiliation find deeper expression in environments of symbiosis.

- Emotional Intelligence, Servant Leadership, and Transformational Leadership are not replaced, but refined through the relational dynamics of Symbiotic Relationship Theory™.

The goal of this chapter is not to discard what has come before but to elevate the conversation. Symbiotic Relationship Theory™ does not compete; it complements. It offers a framework in which the best of classical leadership theory is not only preserved but also brought into deeper alignment with the complex, interconnected nature of human experience.

In the pages ahead, we will:

- Define each classical theory and its core assumptions
- Identify where SRT/SWM aligns, diverges, and enhances the model
- Demonstrate how mutual growth, reciprocity, and emotional safety are not optional, but essential to modern leadership.

By the end of this chapter, you will discover how Symbiotic Relationship Theory™ and the Symbiotic Workplace Model™ present a new approach to leadership and enhance how you engage in relationships with others. Whether you are leading a company, raising a family, managing a team, or cultivating a community, these models provide guidance for creating something enduring.

3.1 Introducing Symbiotic Relationship Theory™ (SRT) and Symbiotic Workplace Model™ (SWM)

The heart of this book is a simple yet transformative truth: human flourishing is relational. Leadership, personal growth, and organizational health do not occur in isolation; they emerge through intentional, mutual investment among people. This is the core concept behind the Symbiotic Relationship Theory™ (SRT) and its organizational counterpart, the Symbiotic Workplace Model™ (SWM).

Traditional leadership theories often explore individual behavior, motivation, and organizational productivity. However, they rarely address the relational environments that can foster or hinder growth, trust, and purpose. In this context, SRT and SWM present a fresh perspective, introducing a model where thriving relationships are built on mutual benefit, shared purpose, accountability, and emotional safety.

3.1.1 What is Symbiotic Relationship Theory™ (SRT)?

Symbiotic Relationship Theory™ (SRT) is a framework for relational leadership and development that emphasizes the importance of **Intentional Interdependence**. It suggests that individuals flourish best when collaborating in environments that promote mutual growth, provide reciprocal value, and foster shared accountability. SRT is based on the biological concept of symbiosis, expanding the idea of mutually beneficial relationships found in nature to human interactions, including families, friends, romantic partners, teams, organizations, and communities. It posits that the most rewarding and fulfilling relationships arise not from one party giving while the other receives but when both parties contribute, share benefits, and grow together. Rather than focusing solely on individual success or compliance with systems, SRT embraces a human-centered growth model that prioritizes emotional safety, trust, collaboration, and transformation instead of domination, hierarchy, or self-interest.

🔑 Core Pillars of SRT

1. **Mutual Growth** – Both parties are committed to learning, evolving, and becoming better through the relationship.
2. **Reciprocity** – Giving and receiving are intentionally balanced and adaptive.
3. **Accountability with Grace** – Every individual is accountable for their impact, and failures are approached with honesty and compassion.
4. **Emotional Safety** – Trust and transparency are cultivated so both people can be fully seen without fear.
5. **Shared Purpose** – The relationship or team is focused on shared goals or purpose.
6. **Adaptability and Feedback** – The system enables adjustments, learning, and repairs in real time.
7. **Recognition and Repair** – Acknowledging positive contributions and addressing relational harm helps restore health.

3.1.2 What is the Symbiotic Workplace Model™ (SWM)?

The Symbiotic Workplace Model™ (SWM) applies SRT to organizational leadership, team dynamics, and workplace culture. It rejects the traditional top-down management approach, fostering an ecosystem based on shared responsibility, trust, and continuous co-advancement. Instead of considering employees as resources to be managed or optimized, SWM recognizes each team member as a relational contributor whose well-being, voice, and vision are vital to the overall health of the organization. SWM creates a work environment where psychological safety, cross-functional collaboration, and mutual recognition are vital to long-term performance and retention.

🔗 Core Components of SWM

1. **Leader as Facilitator, Not Enforcer** – Leadership empowers rather than dominates.
2. **Collaborative Purpose Alignment** – Teams understand and contribute to shared goals.
3. **Reciprocal Feedback Culture** – Honest feedback flows in all directions: upward, downward, and sideways.
4. **Psychological Safety at Scale** – Employees feel secure enough to speak up, take calculated risks, and innovate.
5. **Cross-Functional Accountability** – Teams take shared ownership for outcomes.
6. **Recognition Culture** – Wins are celebrated, and contributions are publicly honored.
7. **Conflict Recovery Protocols** – Conflict is addressed early, respectfully, and constructively.

3.1.3 The Difference Between SRT and Classical Theories

Classical Theories	SRT/SWM Advancement
Focus on individual motivation (Maslow, McClelland)	Emphasizes mutual development and interdependence
Control vs. trust models (McGregor X/Y)	Establishes co-accountability with empathy
Servant leadership	Decentralized service: both parties serve and elevate each other
Emotional intelligence	Applies EQ systemically: from internal mastery to relational culture

3.1.4 Why a Symbiotic Relationship Theory™ & Symbiotic Workplace Model™ Is Needed

In today's society, relationships are strained, teams feel exhausted, families have drifted apart, and leaders often find themselves alone. What we require is not additional control or charisma but rather connection. We need a leadership model that sees leadership not as exerting authority but as a commitment to supporting others. The Symbiotic Relationship Theory™ and the Symbiotic Workplace Model™ provide a framework that honors human dignity, promotes mutual empowerment, and fosters cultures where individuals and organizations can thrive together. As we progress through this chapter, we will examine how SRT and SWM align with, challenge, and expand upon the classical leadership theories that have influenced the past century and discuss why symbiosis must shape the next one.

3.2 Comparison: SRT vs. Maslow's Hierarchy of Needs

Maslow's Hierarchy of Needs, introduced in 1943 by psychologist Abraham Maslow, is a foundational theory in psychology and leadership that continues to be influential today. This model suggests that human motivation is organized into a series of hierarchical stages, beginning with basic physiological needs such as food, water, and shelter. After these essential requirements are satisfied, individuals can move on to higher levels of needs, which include safety and security, social connections, esteem, and ultimately, self-actualization.

Self-actualization represents the highest level of Maslow's hierarchy, where individuals seek personal growth, fulfillment, and the realization of their potential. This framework illustrates that fulfilling lower-level needs is essential for individuals to pursue higher aspirations and highlights the importance of understanding human motivation in both personal development and effective functioning leadership. By recognizing where individuals stand in this hierarchy, leaders can cultivate environments that promote growth and motivation, thereby enhancing overall productivity and satisfaction. The original five layers (with an additional sixth layer added: self-transcendence) include:

1. **Physiological** (food, water, shelter)
2. **Safety** (personal and financial security)
3. **Love and Belonging** (relationships, connection)

4. **Esteem** (achievement, respect)
5. **Self-actualization** (personal growth, potential)
6. **Self-Transcendence** (service beyond self)

This model revolutionized how leaders and educators understand motivation. Yet, as the modern world evolves, so too must our understanding of human development. While Maslow offered a valuable internal lens, Symbiotic Relationship Theory™ (SRT) provides a relational perspective, shifting the focus from individual ascent to mutual elevation.

3.2.1 Where Maslow Ends, SRT Begins

Maslow's hierarchy of needs offers a structure highlighting the sequential satisfaction of individual needs essential for personal development and well-being. Maslow posits that individuals must initially fulfill their fundamental physiological needs- like food, water, and safety- before they can seek higher-level psychological needs, including love, esteem, and ultimately, self-actualization. This model indicates a linear progression in individual growth, suggesting that advancement to higher needs is contingent upon adequately meeting foundational requirements.

In contrast, the Symbiotic Relationship Theory™ (SRT) offers a deeper examination of human interactions by asking, "What happens when several individuals strive to flourish together?" This theory highlights that the dynamics of human relationships operate in a more intricate and interconnected manner. Unlike Maslow's model, SRT recognizes that people's needs are not always satisfied in a strict sequence. In everyday life, individuals may simultaneously give and receive love, provide safety and support to others, and pursue personal growth, even when their lower-level needs are not fully satisfied.

For instance, a parent might give up their own comfort to ensure their child's emotional security, all while dealing with their own unmet needs for social interaction or personal satisfaction. This dual involvement illustrates the interdependence found in relationships and suggests that individuals can prosper on multiple levels at once. Thus, SRT provides a more comprehensive viewpoint that captures the complexities of human relationships, where the pursuit of individual and collective well-being frequently overlaps and intertwines.

3.2.2 SRT's Relational Expansion of Maslow's Categories

Maslow's Category	SRT Expansion
Physiological	Shared resources, care, and provision through relationships
Safety	Emotional and relational safety, not just physical security
Love & Belonging	Reciprocal connection, trust, and interdependence
Esteem	Not just self-esteem, but mutual recognition and respect
Self-Actualization	Achieved *through* relationships, not after them
Self-Transcendence	Embodied in symbiotic service, mentorship, and generational investment

Symbiotic Relationship Theory™ (SRT) does not negate Maslow; rather, it complements it by embedding growth within relational ecosystems instead of isolated individuals.

3.2.3 Leadership Application: Maslow vs. SRT in the Workplace

Maslow's View:

Managers should prioritize meeting employees' fundamental needs, such as pay and safety, before expecting enhanced performance or innovation.

Symbiotic Relationship Theory™ View:

Meeting needs is important, but the quality of relationships among leaders, peers, and teams plays a key role in determining how long employees stay, how much they contribute, and how deeply they engage.

- ✅ A well-paid employee in a toxic work environment will often disengage.
- ✅ A moderately compensated employee in a trust-filled, reciprocal team will often outperform expectations.

Chapter 3.2 Summary: SRT vs. Maslow's Hierarchy of Needs

Maslow highlighted the importance of human needs by presenting a hierarchy that ranks motivators from basic physiological needs to self-actualization. In contrast, Symbiotic Relationship Theory™ (SRT) offers a wider perspective, proposing that human relationships hold equal or even greater significance in comprehending motivation and behavior. While Maslow's model emphasizes the "what" of human needs, SRT investigates the "how," examining the patterns and processes that shape human connections and interactions.

When applied to contexts such as families, organizations, and communities, Symbiotic Relationship Theory™ (SRT) transcends the mere fulfillment of individual needs. It provides a transformative framework that encourages deeper connections and collaboration, fostering an environment where relationships are nurtured and valued. This shift from individualistic needs to collective well-being can enhance cooperation, empathy, and resilience within groups, making SRT a valuable tool for personal growth and societal development.

3.3 SRT/SWM vs. McGregor's Theory X and Theory Y

Douglas McGregor's Theory X and Theory Y, introduced in the 1960s, provided a pivotal shift in management thinking by contrasting two fundamental approaches to employee motivation and behavior. Theory X assumes that people are inherently lazy, require constant supervision, and avoid responsibility. Theory Y, in contrast, posits that people are self-motivated, seek purpose, and will take initiative when given the opportunity.

These two models have greatly influenced leadership practices in the workplace, with Theory X promoting command-and-control settings and Theory Y encouraging trust-oriented, autonomy-focused cultures. McGregor's insights were crucial in pushing leaders to reconsider their beliefs about individuals. Nonetheless, both approaches, despite their strength, offer a binary perspective that does not adequately reflect the complex and relational aspects of human behavior.

The Symbiotic Relationship Theory™ (SRT) and the Symbiotic Workplace Model™ (SWM) provide an intricate and broad framework for examining workplace dynamics. In contrast to conventional methods that mainly concentrate on either management viewpoints or employee actions separately, these models focus on the relational ecosystem involving all participants. This perspective underscores the vital role of mutual trust, which establishes a basis for successful communication and collaboration.

Shared accountability is essential for motivating both managers and employees to recognize their roles within the organization. This collaborative spirit fosters a culture of empowerment, encouraging individuals to support one another. As a result, team cohesion and overall productivity are significantly enhanced.

Shifting the focus to these interdependent relationships, the Symbiotic Relationship Theory™ and the Symbiotic Workplace Model™ not only promote individual growth but also drive collective success, fostering an environment where innovation and adaptability can flourish. Essentially, these frameworks advocate for a holistic understanding of workplace interactions, encouraging organizations to nurture and maintain a symbiotic culture that benefits all involved.

3.3.1 From Assumption to Interaction

McGregor's Question:

What do you believe about people?

SRT/SWM's Question:

How do your relationships shape how people behave?

Instead of adopting a fixed mindset that labels individuals as either lazy or motivated, the Symbiotic Relationship Theory™ (SRT) and the Symbiotic Workplace Model™ (SWM) provide a nuanced framework for understanding interpersonal relationships. These theories highlight the importance of the relational environment in which individuals function, asserting that people's performance and well-being are greatly influenced by the quality of the connections they develop with others.

By analyzing factors such as trust, communication, and collaboration within the workplace, Symbiotic Relationship Theory™ (SRT) and the Symbiotic Workplace Model™ (SWM) highlight that a supportive and mutually beneficial relational climate can foster growth and motivation, while a toxic environment can lead to stagnation and decline. This perspective encourages a shift from labeling individuals to fostering an atmosphere that enhances collective success and personal fulfillment.

✅ A disengaged employee in a Theory X setting may appear unmotivated—but they may simply be unvalued, unheard, or untrusted.

✅ A reluctant team member in a Theory Y setting may still struggle if there is a lack of structure, feedback, or emotional support safety.

Symbiotic Relationship Theory™ (SRT) and the Symbiotic Workplace Model™ (SWM) provide a relationally adaptive middle ground: they build relationships that inspire motivation while allowing for accountability and repair when trust is breached or performance falters. These models emphasize the importance of cultivating connections that not only inspire motivation among team members but also promote a sense of belonging and accountability. In this setting, when trust falters or performance dips, these frameworks promote proactive strategies for restoration and resolution. By emphasizing open communication, mutual support, and shared objectives, organizations can foster a vibrant environment that encourages both personal development and collective achievements. Therefore, SRT and SWM are vital tools for navigating the complexities of workplace relationships, ultimately promoting a more resilient and collaborative organizational culture.

3.3.2 Key Comparison Points

Category	Theory X	Theory Y	SRT/SWM
View of People	Distrustful: People avoid work and must be controlled	Trusting: People are naturally motivated and responsible	Relational: People reflect the health of the environment
Leadership Style	Command-and-control	Empowerment and autonomy	Facilitative leadership, mutual growth, and co-accountability
Feedback Culture	Top-down only	Limited upward flow	Multidirectional: feedback flows up, down, and across
Structure	Rigid, rule-based	Flexible but may lack accountability	Flexible with boundaries, built on trust, repair, and clear expectations
Motivation	Avoid pain or punishment	Seek purpose and autonomy	Grow through reciprocity, trust, and belonging

3.3.3 SRT/SWM's Contribution: Beyond Binary

McGregor's Theory X and Theory Y encouraged leaders to reassess their views on employee motivation and management practices. Theory X assumes that individuals are naturally lazy and need constant oversight, whereas Theory Y indicates that people are driven by intrinsic motivation and can be relied upon to show initiative. In contrast, the Symbiotic Relationship Theory™ (SRT) presents a more comprehensive perspective by fundamentally changing the dialogue regarding leadership and organizational processes.

Instead of merely choosing between differing views on employee behavior, Symbiotic Relationship Theory™ (SRT) urges leaders to create a supportive and nurturing ecosystem where both individuals and the organization can thrive. This involves encouraging open communication, cooperation, and a collective sense of purpose among all team members in the organization. In this way, leaders can cultivate an environment that enhances productivity and meets the varied needs and strengths of their team members, ultimately resulting in a more resilient and adaptable organization.

Rather than labeling people, Symbiotic Relationship Theory™ (SRT) asks:

What conditions are necessary for this person to thrive in a relationship with others?

The Symbiotic Workplace Model™ (SWM) asks:

Which systems encourage relational accountability, emotional safety, and mutual responsibility in the workplace?

This approach shifts the leadership focus from asking, "How do I get people to perform?" to exploring, *"How do we create environments that build purpose, collaboration, and repair when things break down?"*

3.3.4 Theory X and Y Comparison to SRT/SWM

Traditional Theory X Example:

A sales manager relies on constant micromanagement, monitoring software, and rigid quotas. While performance may be achieved in the short term, employee morale suffers, and turnover rates rise.

Theory Y Example:

A start-up founder grants the team unlimited paid time off, eliminates formal reporting structures, and promotes complete autonomy. While some team members excel in this environment, the absence of accountability results in missed targets and unclear expectations.

SRT/SWM Application:

A devoted leader fosters meaningful connections with every member of the team, taking the time to understand their unique strengths and aspirations. Weekly feedback sessions are thoughtfully conducted, creating an open dialogue that encourages personal and professional growth. Together, the leader and team members collaboratively design individual development plans that align with both personal goals and organizational objectives.

In this environment, mutual accountability thrives on a culture of peer recognition, celebrating achievements, and acknowledging contributions. Clear Key Performance Indicators (KPIs) offer guidance, ensuring everyone has clarity and direction while fostering a collective sense of purpose. This approach illustrates the Symbiotic Relationship Theory™: a harmonious blend of empowerment and responsibility, where grace is strategically balanced with restraint. Trust is something cultivated, not simply granted; it thrives on genuine relationships and purposeful engagement, fostering a strong team dynamic built on mutual respect and teamwork.

Chapter 3.3 Summary: SRT/SWM vs. McGregor's Theory X and Theory Y

McGregor played a crucial role in helping leaders understand the fundamental idea that people should not be seen as mere machines. Instead, he emphasized the importance of recognizing the complex human experience. The Symbiotic Relationship Theory™ further elaborates on this concept, illustrating how individuals are deeply influenced by their relational environments. This theory suggests that the interactions and connections people have with one another shape their perspectives, behaviors, and overall well-being, highlighting the intricate web of relationships that contribute to the complexities within an organization.

Theory X and Theory Y offer insights into varying employee behaviors, whereas the Symbiotic Relationship Theory™ and Symbiotic Workplace Model™ highlight the significance of fostering positive interactions and teamwork. These ideas nurture an environment conducive to individual growth, resulting in improved creativity, productivity, and overall workplace well-being. By emphasizing the connections among team members, these models promote a culture that maximizes everyone's potential.

- Theory X isolates performance from trust.
- Theory Y celebrates autonomy but may overlook the need for feedback and structure.
- The Symbiotic Relationship Theory™ and the Symbiotic Workplace Model™ integrate both by embedding leadership within relationships founded on reciprocity, emotional safety, and mutual accountability.

3.4 SRT vs. McClelland's Needs Theory

David McClelland's Needs Theory, commonly known as the "Three Needs Theory," offers a psychological framework for examining human motivation, especially in the workplace context. McClelland suggests that three fundamental needs drive individuals: Achievement, Affiliation, and Power. Each of these needs plays a crucial role in shaping behavior and affecting performance in unique and significant ways. Together, they interact to create a complex motivational landscape that influences how individuals set goals, build relationships, and exert influence in their surroundings. By understanding these fundamental motivations, employers and leaders can better tailor their management strategies to foster engagement, satisfaction, and productivity within their teams. According to McClelland, each of the three fundamental needs influences behavior and performance in unique ways.

1. **Need for Achievement (nAch):** This need signifies a person's aspiration to establish and achieve ambitious goals. Individuals with a heightened need for achievement are typically motivated by their personal standards of excellence and a deep

ambition to tackle intricate challenges. They thrive in environments that provide feedback and enable them to demonstrate their skills. Their commitment to success often drives innovation and outstanding performance as they continually pursue improvement and excellence.

2. **Need for Affiliation (nAff):** This need highlights the significance of social connections and a sense of belonging. People motivated by the need for affiliation cherish close, friendly ties with others and are inspired by the wish to promote teamwork and collaboration. They typically emphasize harmony and consensus in groups, pursuing supportive interactions and steering clear of conflict. Such individuals can play a crucial role in positions that demand strong interpersonal skills and a collaborative attitude, greatly enhancing team dynamics.

3. **Need for Power (nPow):** The need for power relates to the wish to influence, lead, and impact others. Individuals with a strong power need to control their surroundings and inspire or guide others toward specific objectives. This desire can take two forms: personalized power, where individuals seek power for personal gain, and socialized power, which focuses on uplifting and empowering others. Leaders with a significant need for power can drive strategic vision and motivate their teams, but they need to balance their dominance with accountability and ethical considerations.

McClelland's theory highlights the intricate nature of human motivation, revealing that no single motivational strategy can effectively address the needs of every individual within an organization. By comprehending these diverse requirements, leaders and managers can implement personalized management styles that boost employee engagement and satisfaction. Identifying whether team members are chiefly driven by achievement, affiliation, or power allows organizations to better structure teams and roles, fostering an environment that cultivates a range of talents and motivations. This essential understanding has played a crucial role in shaping modern management practices and collaborative strategies.

Yet, Symbiotic Relationship Theory™ (SRT) extends this framework by asking:

What happens when motivation is not just internal but shaped by the health of our relationships?

According to Symbiotic Relationship Theory™ (SRT), motivation is not just an individual trait; it stems from complex interactions between individuals and their environments. People do not reach goals, form relationships, or exert influence in isolation. Their successes and challenges are heavily influenced by the quality of their connections with others and the situations they navigate.

Symbiotic Relationship Theory™ (SRT) emphasizes motivation as a collective experience shaped by both individual and shared factors. It shifts the perspective on motivation from a solo endeavor to a dependent stimulation that arises from the interactions of the relationships people cultivate. By highlighting the importance of these connections, SRT reveals how the strength and quality of relationships can significantly enhance or diminish personal motivation, offering deeper insights into human behavior within social environments.

3.4.1 Side-by-Side Comparison: Needs Theory & Symbiotic Relationship Theory™

Element	McClelland's Needs Theory	Symbiotic Relationship Theory™ (SRT)
Core Focus	Individual psychological needs	Relational ecosystems that cultivate growth
View of Motivation	Internal drivers (achievement, affiliation, power)	Co-created through feedback, trust, and mutual investment
Key Assumption	People have dominant needs influencing behavior	People's needs evolve based on the relational environment
Application	Tailor management style to personality	Transform relational structure to elevate all contributors
Leadership Focus	Adapt to individual needs for engagement	Co-lead with relational integrity, empathy, and shared purpose

3.4.2 Interdependence Reframes the Three Needs

🏆 **Need for Achievement → *Mutual Growth in SRT***

The Symbiotic Relationship Theory™ (SRT) encourages personal achievement without undermining others. In a symbiotic framework, success is gauged not only by individual goals accomplished but also by the number of people who advance alongside you. Achievement is collaborative rather than isolated.

✅ **Example:** A leader's performance is assessed not only by achieving KPIs but also by the number of team members they have coached into promotions or developed through mentoring.

👥 **Need for Affiliation → *Reciprocal Belonging in SRT***

While McClelland's Needs Theory centers on an individual's desire for connection, Symbiotic Relationship Theory™ (SRT) highlights mutual relational responsibility. Belonging involves not only being accepted but also contributing to a safe, uplifting, and empowering environment.

✅ **Example:** A team culture that fosters genuine vulnerability, celebrates collective victories, and supports one another through challenges, driven by authentic care rather than obligation.

🗣 **Need for Power → *Influence as Stewardship in SRT***

Symbiotic Relationship Theory™ (SRT) does not reject power; rather, it redefines it. Influence is not defined by control or prestige; it focuses on empowering others to grow. Leadership evolves into a relational role characterized by stewardship and service.

✅ **Example:** A Symbiotic Leader™ (SL) uses their position not to control but to uplift others, often and transparently delegating, mentoring, and recognizing their contributions.

3.4.3 SRT in the Workplace vs. Individual Motivation Models

McClelland's model emphasizes the importance of managers recognizing the diverse motivational profiles of their team members, enabling them to tailor their strategies to meet individual needs. Conversely, the Symbiotic Relationship Theory™ (SRT) and the Symbiotic Workplace Model™ (SWM) promote a more comprehensive transformation of the workplace environment as a whole. These frameworks suggest that by fostering a supportive and flexible organizational culture, managers can establish conditions where individuals motivated by achievement, affiliation, or power can both coexist and flourish. This strategy acknowledges the relationship between personal motivations and the larger workplace environment, emphasizing the need for settings that promote collaboration, engagement, and personal development for all participants.

- High achievers require both clarity and collaboration.
- Affiliators require not only social bonds but also emotional safety and respect.
- Power-seekers require purpose and the opportunity to influence with integrity.

McClelland offers a useful diagnostic tool to explore individual behaviors and motivations, whereas the Symbiotic Relationship Theory™ (SRT) adopts a broader ecosystem strategy that centers on collaborative interactions. In contrast to McClelland's focus on personal achievements and motivations, SRT is concerned with fostering mutual relationships between individuals, groups, or organizations. This approach aims to create environments that support collective growth and enhance connections that yield shared achievements, a sense of belonging, and a strong purpose. By prioritizing healthy interactions, SRT highlights the significance of interdependence in promoting collective well-being, which becomes a valuable outcome of the relationships nurtured within the ecosystem.

Chapter 3.4 Summary: SRT vs. McClelland's Needs Theory

McClelland demonstrated that individuals are motivated by factors beyond financial gain and mere survival; they seek meaning, a sense of belonging, and the desire to make an impact. Symbiotic Relationship Theory™ (SRT) supports this idea while expanding on it further. In the Symbiotic Workplace Model™ (SWM), motivation arises as a collective experience rather than just an individual trait, nurtured by collaborative structures, emotional safety, and shared purpose.

In Symbiotic Relationship Theory™ (SRT) and Symbiotic Workplace Model™ (SWM):

- Achievement is shared, not hoarded.
- Belonging is mutual, not one-sided.
- Power is used to lift others, not control them.

3.5 SRT/SWM and Emotional Intelligence (Goleman)

In his groundbreaking exploration of Emotional Intelligence (EQ), Daniel Goleman significantly changed the perception of leadership and organizational behavior. He shifted the focus away from traditional measures of Intelligence Quotient (IQ) and technical skills, highlighting the importance of emotional intelligence in effective leadership. Goleman pinpointed five crucial competencies vital for successful leaders: self-awareness, self-regulation, motivation, empathy, and social skills. These competencies enhance a leader's ability to connect with others, motivate teams, and create a supportive work atmosphere, ultimately fostering organizational success. Instead of regarding intelligence solely as IQ or technical capability, Goleman emphasized these five core competencies as essential for effective leadership.

1. **Self-Awareness** – Recognizing one's own emotions
2. **Self-Regulation** – Managing emotions and impulses
3. **Motivation** – Harnessing passion to pursue goals with persistence
4. **Empathy** – Understanding others' emotional makeup
5. **Social Skills** – Managing relationships and building networks

Goleman's model highlights that while technical skills are important, they represent only a small part of what contributes to a leader's overall success. The true differentiators between exceptional leaders and their average counterparts often lie in their emotional intelligence. This includes the ability to effectively regulate one's own emotions, cultivate deep empathy for the feelings and needs of others, and foster strong relational trust within teams. Such interpersonal skills not only create a harmonious work environment but also inspire loyalty, collaboration, and high performance among team members.

While Emotional Intelligence (EQ) has emerged as a critical element in modern leadership development, it often focuses on an individualistic perspective, primarily analyzing the leader's internal thoughts and feelings. In contrast, Symbiotic Relationship Theory™ (SRT) and the Symbiotic Workplace Model™ (SWM) build upon Daniel Goleman's foundational concepts by introducing a more relational and systemic approach to emotional intelligence. These frameworks highlight the relationship between team interactions and organizational culture, demonstrating that effective leadership requires both individual emotional awareness and the fostering of collaborative relationships alongside a supportive work environment. By embracing SRT and SWM, leaders can develop a comprehensive understanding of EQ that fosters both personal growth and collective success within their organizations.

3.5.1 EQ vs. SRT: From Inward Reflection to Relational Culture

Emotional Intelligence (EQ)	Symbiotic Relationship Theory™ (SRT)
Focuses on individual emotional awareness and control	Focuses on the relational environment that cultivates trust, growth, and emotional safety
Strengthens interpersonal skills of a leader	Multiplies those skills into scalable behaviors across teams and organizations
Builds empathy and influence	Builds reciprocity, mutual accountability, and cultural empathy
Requires introspection and maturity	Requires intentional investment in relational systems

Where EQ is a mirror, SRT is a network.
Where EQ strengthens the leader, SRT strengthens the whole.

3.5.2 How SRT/SWM Operationalize Emotional Intelligence

✅ Self-Awareness → Shared Awareness

The Symbiotic Relationship Theory™ (SRT) expands the focus of personal reflection, transforming it into a comprehensive evaluation of collaborative relationships. The Symbiotic Workplace Model™ (SWM) promotes psychological safety by establishing transparent and accessible feedback channels. This method allows leaders to engage in authentic and compassionate conversations, fostering collective growth rooted in mutual understanding and shared awareness among team members.

Example: A symbiotic team conducts regular "pulse check" meetings, during which emotional tension, morale, and misalignment are discussed openly and constructively.

✅ Self-Regulation → Systemic Grace

Instead of relying entirely on one leader to manage their impulses, the Symbiotic Relationship Theory™ (SRT) nurtures an organizational culture that values shared responsibility and empathy. This framework encourages open acknowledgment of mistakes, creating a safe space where individuals are motivated to learn and develop. The emphasis on restoration and reconciliation promotes emotional maturity across the organization. As a result, this approach not only fortifies relationships among team members but also boosts overall resilience and adaptability, ultimately fostering a more unified and innovative workplace.

Example: When a conflict arises, the Symbiotic Workplace Model™ (SWM) ensures it is resolved through restorative processes instead of blame games.

- **Motivation → Purpose-Driven Mutuality**

In Symbiotic Relationship Theory™ (SRT) and the Symbiotic Workplace Model™ (SWM), motivation transcends individual goals; it is cultivated through a shared vision and contributions. The organization creates significance through mutual purpose, encouraging individuals to strive not only for personal achievement but also for the success of the community as a whole.

Example: Frontline workers recognize how their performance aligns with the C-suite's vision, as communication is clear, transparent, and aligned with values.

- **Empathy → Cultural Emotional Intelligence**

Empathy within Symbiotic Relationship Theory™ (SRT) transcends simple comprehension; it evolves into an actionable framework. This framework influences various organizational areas, such as policy formulation, meeting formats, conflict management strategies, and employee onboarding practices. The Symbiotic Workplace Model™ (SWM) integrates empathy as a core component of the organizational structure, ensuring it is deeply embedded in workplace interactions rather than relying solely on individual traits. This approach fosters a culture of shared empathy, enhancing collaboration and mutual respect among team members.

Example: Leaders create workflows that accommodate different cognitive styles, personal crises, and emotional bandwidth, exhibiting cultural empathy.

Social Skills → Embedded Relational Norms

Rather than depending solely on personal charisma or natural social intuition, the Symbiotic Workplace Model™ (SWM) weaves structured trust-building actions and established rituals into the foundation of team norms and organizational processes. This method guarantees the intentional and ongoing cultivation of trust, promoting a collaborative atmosphere where every member feels appreciated and engaged. By integrating these practices into everyday interactions, the SWM fosters a lasting culture of trust that boosts teamwork and productivity.

Example: Recognition systems, transparent communication channels, and inclusive decision-making become part of the operating rhythm, not just leader-driven habits.

Chapter 3.5 Summary: SRT/SWM and Emotional Intelligence (Goleman)

Emotional Intelligence revolutionized leadership by shifting the focus from a purely mechanical approach to one that prioritizes human connections and emotional awareness. Building on this foundation, the concepts of Symbiotic Relationship Theory™ and the Symbiotic Workplace Model™ elevate this transformation even further. They integrate emotional well-being into the very fabric of relational systems and organizational culture, fostering environments where collaboration, empathy, and mutual growth thrive. This comprehensive approach not only enhances individual performance but also cultivates a resilient and engaged workforce that is better equipped to navigate the complexities of modern organizational life.

- Emotional Intelligence (EQ) makes better leaders.
- Symbiotic Relationship Theory™ (SRT) builds better teams, relationships, and cultures.
- Symbiotic Workplace Model™ (SWM) ensures that emotional intelligence is not a trait but a framework.

The Symbiotic Relationship Theory™ (SRT) and the Symbiotic Workplace Model™ (SWM) are essential frameworks that foster individual and collective growth while incorporating compassion, accountability, and relational depth within organizational culture. These ideas promote a comprehensive approach to interactions, emphasizing the deep interconnectedness that encourages empathy and understanding among team members. By embedding these values into the organizational structure, SRT and SWM cultivate an environment where trust and responsibility flourish, resulting in more meaningful and productive workplace collaborations.

3.6 SRT vs. Servant Leadership

Servant Leadership, a concept introduced by Robert Greenleaf in the 1970s, fundamentally transformed the traditional understanding of leadership by inverting the conventional power hierarchy. Instead of a top-down approach characterized by command and control, servant leaders emphasize the importance of prioritizing the needs of others. This leadership style empowers team members, fosters personal and professional growth, and encourages collaborative decision-making.

Servant leaders demonstrate key qualities such as humility, active listening, empathy, and a deep dedication to serving others. They make a concerted effort to grasp the viewpoints and difficulties experienced by their team, fostering an atmosphere where all members feel appreciated and acknowledged. By embodying these traits, servant leaders build trust and loyalty, encouraging a culture of inclusivity and engagement. This method boosts team performance and fosters a more ethical and compassionate organizational environment.

The servant leader is:

- A listener before a speaker
- A steward before a commander
- A guide before a boss

The Symbiotic Relationship Theory™ (SRT) and the Symbiotic Workplace Model™ (SWM) expand upon the foundational principles of servant leadership by transforming the concept from a primarily leader-centric approach to one that emphasizes mutual, relational empowerment at all levels of the organization. While servant leadership focuses mainly on the attitude and behavior of the leader in serving their team, SRT adopts a broader perspective by decentralizing traditional notions of leadership influence.

This shift promotes the distribution of relational responsibility, fostering a more collaborative environment within the organization. This framework transforms leadership into a shared responsibility that encourages open communication and trust among members. Ultimately, this method boosts individual and organizational performance through collective growth and support.

3.6.1 Core Comparison: Servant Leadership vs. Symbiotic Relationship Theory™

Element	Servant Leadership	Symbiotic Relationship Theory™ (SRT)
Leadership Focus	The leader serves the needs of the team	All individuals serve and elevate each other through mutual growth
Power Distribution	Leader lowers themselves to raise others	Power is relationally distributed; leadership influence is shared

Cultural Impact	Driven by the leader's character and example	Driven by relational structure, shared feedback, and accountability
Growth Model	Leader empowers others	Entire team co-develops through reciprocal investment
Organizational Reach	Often tied to a humble leader	System-wide model; culture doesn't rely on one person's humility

3.6.2 From Leader-Centric to Ecosystemic

Servant Leadership says:

"The leader must serve for others to grow."

Symbiotic Relationship Theory™ (SRT) says:

"Everyone must serve and grow together."

In various applications of servant leadership, a team's well-being is intricately connected to the leader's integrity and self-awareness. However, this raises important questions: What happens when the leader changes? How can an organization maintain its culture if it hasn't been deeply integrated into its core beliefs and practices?

This is where the Symbiotic Relationship Theory™ (SRT) and the Symbiotic Workplace Model™ (SWM) come into play, offering a framework that establishes a lasting legacy in organizational culture. These theories reframe relational leadership, shifting its focus from being merely an individual virtue to fostering a collective ecosystem. Within this ecosystem, principles such as grace, accountability, and empowerment are not solely reliant on individual personalities. Instead, they become embedded within the organization's policies, culture, and overall behavior.

By embracing Symbiotic Relationship Theory™ (SRT) and the Symbiotic Workplace Model™ (SWM), organizations can create a robust environment where positive relationships flourish, regardless of changes in leadership. This approach encourages a sustainable and resilient culture that empowers all members of the organization, ensuring that the values of servant leadership are preserved and propagated throughout the fabric of the organization.

3.6.3 Practical Application

Scenario	Servant Leadership	SRT/SWM
Onboarding a new employee	The leader ensures their integration and support	Team takes ownership; cross-training, mentorship, and psychological safety are shared responsibilities
Addressing conflict	The leader mediates with humility and wisdom	The team operates with agreed-upon conflict recovery protocols, where ownership, repair, and restoration are normalized
Driving innovation	The leader creates space for creative voices	Innovation emerges through reciprocal feedback loops, safety to fail, and shared ideation practices

| **Scaling culture** | Relies on presence of servant-minded leaders | Built into systems, rituals, and rhythms; not dependent on charisma or individual traits |

Chapter 3.6 Summary: SRT vs. Servant Leadership

Servant Leadership is foundational, but Symbiotic Relationship Theory™ (SRT) and the Symbiotic Workplace Model™ (SWM) are the next evolution.

- Servant leadership focuses on the leader's humility.
- SRT/SWM focuses on every person's relational responsibility.
- Servant leadership inspires team health.
- SRT/SWM institutionalize relational health and mutual elevation.

By expanding on the concepts of servant leadership into a comprehensive, systemic model, Symbiotic Leadership™ offers a framework designed to cultivate a culture focused on shared values and collective development. This methodology emphasizes the importance of service, empowerment, and transformation in a way that is both scalable and sustainable over time.

In this model, leaders emphasize building collaboration and mutual support within their organizations, ensuring that every member feels appreciated and empowered to engage in the shared mission. By prioritizing the needs of both individuals and the community, Symbiotic Leadership™ fosters an atmosphere where innovation flourishes and personal growth is central to the organization's success. Ultimately, this framework places service at the heart of leadership, generating a transformative influence that resonates across the entire organization and beyond.

3.7: Chapter Summary – Reframing the Leadership Conversation?

Throughout this chapter, we explored six foundational theories of leadership and motivation that have greatly influenced our understanding of organizational behavior, personal growth, and team dynamics. From Maslow's Hierarchy of Needs to Servant Leadership, each model offers valuable insights. However, they frequently interpret leadership and motivation through individualistic, hierarchical, or internal perspectives.

Conversely, the Symbiotic Relationship Theory™ (SRT) and the Symbiotic Workplace Model™ (SWM) provide a daring new perspective, positioning leadership not solely within traditional hierarchies or individual development, but in mutual growth, a common goal, and deliberate interdependence. These approaches shift the leadership discourse to focus on the key elements that truly support performance and purpose: relationships.

3.7.1 What We've Learned

- Maslow showed us what people need.
  Symbiotic Relationship Theory (SRT) shows us how needs are fulfilled through healthy, reciprocal relationships.

- McGregor framed motivation through assumptions about people.
  Symbiotic Relationship Theory (SRT) replaces assumption with relational engagement and cultural design.

- McClelland identified what drives people internally.
  Symbiotic Relationship Theory (SRT) reveals how interpersonal relationships activate, nurture, or diminish those drivers.

- Goleman taught us emotional intelligence starts within.
  Symbiotic Relationship Theory (SRT) /Symbiotic Workplace Model (SWM) scale that emotional intelligence into team and cultural architecture.

- Servant Leadership modeled the power of humility.
  Symbiotic Relationship Theory (SRT) /Symbiotic Workplace Model (SWM) operationalize service into ecosystems of mutual care and accountability.

3.7.2 Comparative Overview: Classic Theories vs. SRT/SWM

Framework	Primary Focus	Key Limitation	SRT/SWM Enhancement
Maslow's Hierarchy	Individual needs (self-actualization)	Lacks relational context; linear	Integrates needs within reciprocal relationships
McGregor's Theory X/Y	Assumptions about motivation (control vs. trust)	Binary perspective; limited relational nuance	Replaces binary views with adaptive ecosystems
McClelland's Needs Theory	Achievement, affiliation, power	Isolates internal drivers from environment	Activates needs through mutual support structures
Goleman's Emotional Intelligence	Emotional self-awareness and empathy	Centered on individual leader; lacks system integration	Scale emotional intelligence into team culture
Servant Leadership	Leader's posture of humility and service	Dependent on leader's character; hard to scale	Decentralizes service to build system-wide health
SRT/SWM	Mutual growth through relational ecosystems	None (designed to scale relational health across all levels)	Offers relationally grounded, scalable leadership model

Chapter 3 Closing Thought

In an ever-evolving landscape characterized by shifting values, the rise of remote workforces, and the pervasive threat of cultural burnout, tomorrow's leaders must embody a unique blend of qualities. They must be relationally resilient, fostering strong and meaningful connections, even from a distance. Their emotional intelligence should be finely tuned, enabling them to understand and respond to the feelings and needs of their teams with empathy and insight. Additionally, they should embrace a structurally reciprocal approach, promoting an environment where collaboration and mutual support are encouraged and embedded in the organizational culture. This combination of traits will be essential for navigating the complexities of modern leadership.

The Symbiotic Relationship Theory™ and the Symbiotic Workplace Model™ provide a rich and nuanced framework that transforms our understanding of leadership. This innovative approach highlights the significance of intrinsic motivation and collaborative practices, departing from traditional top-down management styles that often create barriers between leaders and team members. By nurturing an environment that promotes genuine connections and active engagement, this model develops a workforce that is more connected and more invested in their collective success. The outcome is a thriving organization where individuals feel valued and empowered, resulting in enhanced creativity, productivity, and overall job satisfaction.

As we enter the next chapter, we will shift from theoretical concepts to practical applications. We aim to establish a robust and scalable Symbiotic Leadership™ Framework that empowers C-suite executives, middle managers, and frontline employees. This framework will promote the development of healthy, impactful, and aligned organizational cultures at every level. By fostering shared values and collective accountability, we aim to create an environment in which every team member contributes to the overall vision and success of the organization, ultimately driving sustainable growth and innovation.

CHAPTER 4
SYMBIOTIC LEADERSHIP
Scaling Relationship Driven Growth

Chapter 4: Symbiotic Leadership™
Scaling Relationship-Driven Growth

Look into the immense Milky Way Galaxy, where Sagittarius A-Star resides at its core, serving as a powerful gravitational anchor that draws billions of stars into a harmonious dance of stability. This cosmic centerpiece reminds us of the intricate forces that shape our universe. Now, let us zoom in on our solar system, where the sun assumes a similar role, orchestrating the orbits of planets and providing the essential light and energy that sustain life on Earth. Beyond our solar system, this captivating spiral pattern emerges in various forms, from the elegant spirals of seashells and the intricate arrangements of pinecones to the double helix of our DNA.

This is not a coincidence; it reflects a deeper design inherent in nature.

In the field of leadership, Symbiotic Leadership™ reflects this essential universal framework. It goes beyond conventional hierarchies, extending throughout all levels of an organization, from top executives in the C-suite to team members on the front lines. This leadership approach relies on reciprocity, rhythm, and relational alignment principles, which are crucial for cultivating a united and cohesive work environment.

Just as galaxies scale into solar systems and solar systems evolve into complex cellular structures, great leadership flourishes when the patterns of growth, trust, and shared purpose are replicated with integrity at every level of the organization. This reinforces a culture where individuals feel connected to a broader mission and empowered in their roles. This framework offers not just another hierarchical pyramid or rigid matrix but rather a dynamic, living model of a leadership ecosystem that mirrors the elegant order of the universe. It encourages leaders to cultivate relationships and foster connection, creating a vibrant community that thrives on mutual support and adapts and evolves in response to the changing landscape of the world around us.

4.1 The Three Spheres of the Symbiotic Model

1. **Symbiotic Relationship Theory™ (SRT) – The Core of Connection**

   Definition: A theory rooted in mutual growth, shared purpose, emotional safety, and reciprocal accountability.

   Location in the model: The *innermost sphere* where everything begins with the quality of the relationship.

   Role: Defines how people flourish together, personally and professionally.

2. **Symbiotic Workplace Model™ (SWM) – The Relational Ecosystem**

   Definition: The operational expression of SRT within organizations—where systems, culture, and leadership behaviors align.

   Location: The *middle sphere* turns relationship values into culture and process.

Role: Connects people, departments, and strategies through shared feedback, safety, and structure.

3. **Symbiotic Leadership Framework™ (SLF)** – *The Scalable Structure*

Definition: The applied framework that scales Symbiotic Relationship Theory™ (SRT) and Symbiotic Workplace Model™ (SWM) values are applied to teams, departments, and enterprises using 12 recursive principles.

Location: The *outermost sphere*—visible action, structural integrity, and leadership legacy.

Role: Allows any part of the organization to reflect the whole through fractal leadership practices.

4.2 What is Symbiotic Leadership™?

In a landscape where conventional leadership is typically characterized by strict hierarchies, clear authority, or the appealing presence of a charismatic leader, Symbiotic Leadership™ stands out as an innovative framework. This fresh perspective reinterprets leadership as relational stewardship, a complex network that prioritizes collaboration and mutual support. By cultivating a setting where leadership is both scalable and reciprocal, this model promotes active participation from all members within the organization in the collective journey of growth and progress. It represents a deeply involved practice focused on the thriving of individuals and groups, establishing a vibrant ecosystem where joint success is fostered through continuous dialogue and partnership.

In contrast to traditional methods that rely on authority, Symbiotic Leadership™ focuses on creating environments where individuals succeed through meaningful interdependence. This strategy takes cues from the natural equilibrium seen in the universe, where galaxies, ecosystems, and the human body thrive through interconnectedness and a shared sense of purpose. By reflecting this inherent harmony, Symbiotic Leadership™ nurtures an organizational culture that encourages collaboration, empathy, and sustainable growth.

At its essence, Symbiotic Leadership™ centers on the practice of aligning people, systems, and strategies through relationship-based principles. It is based on the foundational concepts of Symbiotic Relationship Theory™ (SRT) and the Symbiotic Workplace Model™ (SWM), which together form a repeatable and scalable framework. This framework not only ensures that every tier of an organization—from the C-Suite to frontline employees- thrives but also empowers individuals to take ownership of their roles and contributions.

Symbiotic Leadership™ fosters a culture of belonging and purpose in organizations through effective communication, shared goals, and collective accountability. It prompts leaders to listen actively, appreciate diverse perspectives, and prioritize the well-being of all stakeholders. This approach transforms leadership into a collaborative journey, shifting growth from a top-down directive to a shared adventure that engages every member of the organization.

4.2.1 Key Characteristics of Symbiotic Leadership™

Trait	Description
Reciprocal	Leadership is a shared exchange, not a one-way street. Leaders grow by helping others grow.
Scalable	The same principles apply to executives, team leads, and individual contributors.
Relationally Rooted	Trust, safety, and emotional intelligence aren't soft skills. They are strategic infrastructure.
Principle-Driven	Leadership decisions are guided by 12 core principles designed to promote health and performance.
Systemically Applied	Culture isn't accidental. Systems, rituals, and policies reflect relational alignment.

4.2.2 Why Symbiotic Leadership™ Is Needed Now

The traditional leadership landscape is crumbling under modern challenges:

- **Burnout is rising**, especially among mid-level leaders.
- **Turnover and disengagement** are at all-time highs.

- **Command-and-control models** stifle innovation and suppress trust.
- **Charismatic leadership**, while appealing, fails to scale and often collapses when the personality departs.

Symbiotic Leadership™ fills these gaps by substituting pressure with purpose, hierarchy with harmony, and control with collaboration. It is both emotionally intelligent and operationally strategic.

Symbiotic Leadership™ is the next evolution of leadership for the modern workplace.
It is:

- Rooted in relationship
- Activated through trust
- Scaled through systems
- Sustained through principles
- Ultimately, it is designed to reflect the order of creation in your organization's culture.

4.2.3 The Relationship to SRT and SWM

Symbiotic Leadership™ represents the visible fruit of Symbiotic Relationship Theory™ (SRT) and Symbiotic Workplace Model™ (SWM):

- **Symbiotic Relationship Theory™ (SRT)** provides the philosophical and behavioral foundation: mutual growth, emotional safety, shared purpose, and accountability with grace.

- **Symbiotic Workplace Model™ (SWM)** translates those behaviors into organizational systems: leadership rhythms, communication strategies, conflict recovery protocols, and distributed influence.
- **Symbiotic Leadership Framework™ (SLF)** operationalizes these ideas into a set of 12 principles, offering a roadmap for everyday leadership decisions and strategic development.

This model enables organizations to establish a unified leadership identity, where their vision and values are consistently reflected at every level of operation.

4.3 The 12 Principles of Symbiotic Leadership™

#	Principle	Concept	Metaphor
1	Mutual Empowerment	Leaders raise others while being raised	Two-way mirror
2	Shared Vision & Purpose	Every role aligns to a central mission	Gravitational orbit
3	Accountability with Grace	Mistakes refine, not destroy	Tuning fork
4	Emotional Safety	Safe spaces produce bold leaders	Oxygenated room
5	Reciprocal Feedback	Feedback loops fuel progress	Echo chamber (healthy)
6	Transparent Communication	Clarity builds trust and resilience	Open water

7	Distributed Leadership	Everyone leads where they stand	Mycelium network
8	Rhythmic Recognition	Celebration sustains momentum	Drums of culture
9	Constructive Conflict	Conflict becomes a catalyst, not a crisis	Fire that purifies
10	Adaptable Alignment	Stay rooted but flexible	Tree in wind
11	Legacy Mindset	Leadership builds beyond now	Ring in a tree
12	Leadership as Stewardship	Leadership is a trust, not a title	Garden caretaker

Principle 1: Mutual Empowerment Over Top-Down Control

Definition:
Symbiotic leaders empower others to lead—not from above, but from alongside. Authority is shared, not hoarded. Growth is measured by how many others you lift as you rise.

Workplace Application:

- Leaders delegate decision-making authority with guidance and trust.
- Empowerment flows across roles—frontline workers are invited into idea generation, process design, and ownership of results.

- Teams build cross-functional partnerships that honor shared responsibility.

Fractal Metaphor:
Like a branch that supports both the fruit and the root, empowerment feeds and is fed by those around it.

Principle 2: Shared Vision and Purpose

Definition:
Symbiotic leaders unify people around a common goal. Vision isn't imposed—it's co-owned. Everyone sees how their part contributes to the whole.

Workplace Application:

- All departments are aligned to a central, meaningful mission.
- Frontline workers can articulate how their role advances organizational impact.
- Vision is revisited regularly and adapted with input from all levels.

Fractal Metaphor:
Like a galaxy's stars rotate in harmony around its gravitational center, vision keeps teams in relational and strategic orbit.

Principle 3: Accountability with Grace

Definition:
Symbiotic Leadership™ cultivates a culture of

responsibility that is never detached from compassion. Failure is a path to restoration, not rejection.

Workplace Application:

- Errors are addressed with clear expectations and follow-up support.
- Peer accountability is encouraged without fear or shame.
- Growth conversations replace punitive discipline.

Fractal Metaphor:
Like pruning a tree to foster stronger growth, accountability removes what's unhelpful to allow flourishing.

Principle 4: Emotional Safety Before Performance Pressure

Definition:
Without emotional safety, innovation, collaboration, and trust collapse. Symbiotic leaders create space for vulnerability, honesty, and psychological security.

Workplace Application:

- Employees feel safe admitting mistakes or asking for help.
- Leaders model emotional transparency and humility.
- Safety is regularly assessed through check-ins, not assumptions.

Fractal Metaphor:
Like oxygen in a room, unseen but essential, emotional safety is the invisible environment that sustains growth.

Principle 5: Reciprocal Feedback Loops

Definition:
Feedback is not a one-way street. In symbiotic cultures, feedback flows up, down, and across. Everyone gives and receives in service of shared growth.

Workplace Application:

- Leaders invite feedback from employees and peers.
- Constructive feedback is normalized in team culture.
- Regular 360 reviews or listening sessions promote shared learning.

Fractal Metaphor:
Like rivers that feed and are fed by smaller streams, feedback sustains the ecosystem when it flows in all directions.

Principle 6: Transparent Communication

Definition:
Clarity builds trust. Symbiotic leaders practice and expect honest, timely, and clear communication, especially in challenging or changing situations.

Workplace Application:

- Strategy, goals, and issues are openly discussed.

- Communication tools and expectations are standardized across departments.
- Leaders eliminate ambiguity by overcommunicating direction and support.

Fractal Metaphor:
Like sunlight passing through glass, clarity illuminates, warms, and guides everything it encounters.

Principle 7: Distributed Leadership

Definition:
Symbiotic Leadership™ thrives when influence is shared. Every person is expected to lead where they are—regardless of title.

Workplace Application:

- Employees are encouraged to take initiative and own results.
- Leadership roles rotate within teams to build depth and perspective.
- Decision-making is collaborative, with clear accountability for outcomes.

Fractal Metaphor:
Like mycelium in a forest, leadership is a network, not a ladder. Every part contributes to the strength of the whole.

Principle 8: Rhythmic Recognition

Definition:
Healthy ecosystems celebrate growth in rhythm. Recognition is not random; it is deliberate, expected, and aligned with values.

Workplace Application:

- Regular recognition rituals (weekly wins, shout-outs, peer-to-peer gratitude)
- Rewards based on collaborative outcomes, not just individual heroics
- Appreciation is both spontaneous and structured

Fractal Metaphor:
Like waves on a shoreline, consistent praise strengthens the land it touches.

Principle 9: Constructive Conflict

Definition:
Conflict is not a disruption—it's a catalyst. In symbiotic cultures, conflict is addressed early and transformed into alignment.

Workplace Application:

- Teams are trained in healthy disagreement and dialogue
- Leaders create space for challenge without defensiveness
- Resolution models (e.g., restorative circles, mediated conversations) are normalized

Fractal Metaphor:
Like fire in a forest, it can either destroy or refine. Constructive conflict clears space for deeper roots.

Principle 10: Adaptable Alignment

Definition:
Symbiotic leaders stay rooted in purpose yet are flexible in approach. They adapt systems without compromising vision.

Workplace Application:

- Structures are reviewed and improved regularly
- Feedback from every level influences operational shifts
- Leaders adjust quickly to environmental, market, or relational changes

Fractal Metaphor:
Like a tree in the wind, flexibility preserves strength without breaking the core.

Principle 11: Legacy Mindset

Definition:
Leadership is generational. Symbiotic leaders build systems that outlast them—developing others, not just hitting metrics.

Workplace Application:

- Succession planning is active and integrated

- Mentorship and talent development are built into the workflow
- Decisions are evaluated for long-term impact on people and purpose

Fractal Metaphor:
Like rings in a tree, true leadership leaves behind visible evidence of growth and endurance.

Principle 12: Sacred Stewardship

Definition:
Leadership is not ownership. It's stewardship. A trust to care for people, vision, and influence with humility and integrity.

Workplace Application:

- Leaders hold their power with responsibility, not entitlement
- Teams treat culture and purpose as a shared trust
- Ethics, empathy, and sustainability guide strategy

Fractal Metaphor:
Like tending a garden, you don't own the growth, but you are responsible for the conditions.

4.4: Application Across Scales

Symbiotic Leadership™ is not bound to a position or department. It is a **scalable pattern**. Just as a fractal maintains its structure from micro to macro, **the 12 Symbiotic**

Leadership™ Principles remain consistent across all organizational levels, adjusting only in scope and responsibility.

Each role, whether C-suite executive, mid-level manager, or frontline contributor, plays a part in **reciprocally sustaining the culture of growth, trust, and accountability**. The framework works best not when isolated to the top, but when **every level embodies its portion of the pattern**.

Below is a practical matrix showing how each principle of Symbiotic Leadership™ is expressed uniquely across the three major layers of an organization:

4.4.1 Symbiotic Leadership Principles Matrix™

Principle	C-Suite Application	Mid-Level Application	Frontline Application
1. Mutual Empowerment	Delegate ownership, develop other leaders	Enable autonomy within teams	Lead from your role; offer input and support
2. Shared Vision & Purpose	Cast a compelling and inclusive vision	Translate vision into team goals	Connect tasks to the bigger picture
3. Accountability w/ Grace	Model responsibility with humility	Hold reports accountable with compassion	Own mistakes and grow from them
4. Emotional Safety	Foster open, inclusive exec culture	Build team environments of psychological safety	Be trustworthy, kind, and emotionally aware

Principle	C-Suite Application	Mid-Level Application	Frontline Application
5. Reciprocal Feedback Loops	Seek upward feedback from VPs, stakeholders	Use 360 feedback processes	Give and receive feedback with maturity
6. Transparent Communication	Communicate transparently across hierarchy	Maintain open team channels (e.g., Slack, check-ins)	Speak clearly, respectfully, and timely
7. Distributed Leadership	Empower cross-functional leadership	Share leadership roles within the team	Take initiative when leadership is needed
8. Rhythmic Recognition	Celebrate strategic wins and team efforts	Create recurring moments of gratitude	Recognize your peers' efforts regularly
9. Constructive Conflict	Address conflict between senior leaders proactively	Resolve tension and clarify expectations early	Engage in healthy conflict and resolution
10. Adaptable Alignment	Pivot strategy while anchoring purpose	Adapt team processes to real-world shifts	Stay flexible and open to change
11. Legacy Mindset	Mentor next-gen execs and preserve the mission	Build skills in others; develop leaders below you	Think long-term and invest in your growth

Principle	C-Suite Application	Mid-Level Application	Frontline Application
12. Sacred Stewardship	Lead with ethics, long-view, and responsibility	Guard culture and values in day-to-day decisions	Treat your work as a mirror of your values

4.5: The Three Layers of the Symbiotic Model

In a vast galaxy, the invisible threads of gravitational force bind billions of shimmering stars, allowing them to dance in harmonious rotation. Similarly, in a dynamic workplace, it is the shared vision that ignites passion, the relational integrity that fosters trust and collaboration, and the steadfast accountability of leadership that weaves together individuals, teams, and strategic goals, creating a cohesive and thriving environment. Symbiotic Leadership™ is not a structured hierarchy; instead, it is a relational system composed of three interconnected and recurring layers:

1. **Symbiotic Relationship Theory™ (SRT)**
2. **Symbiotic Workplace Model™ (SWM)**
3. **Symbiotic Leadership Framework™ (SLF)**

Together, they create a self-similar pattern of leadership that adapts to any level, from executive teams to daily interactions, just as a fractal adapts across scales while maintaining its form.

4.5.1. Symbiotic Relationship Theory™ (SRT)

The Inner Core – The DNA of Human Flourishing

Symbiotic Relationship Theory™ (SRT) is the foundational philosophy that asserts that people thrive through mutual investment. Leadership is not sustainable without emotional safety, reciprocal growth, and shared responsibility. SRT identifies the relational building blocks that make trust scalable and performance sustainable.

Key Pillars of SRT:

- **Mutual Growth**: Everyone elevates together
- **Reciprocity**: Giving and receiving are both expected
- **Accountability with Grace**: Truth and empathy coexist
- **Emotional Safety**: Performance follows belonging
- **Shared Purpose**: Individuals know how they fit in the whole

🔎 **Why it matters**:
Without healthy relationship interactions, even the best systems collapse. SRT provides the ethical and emotional blueprint for leadership at its root.

4.5.2. Symbiotic Workplace Model™ (SWM)

The Relational Ecosystem – Culture in Motion

The Symbiotic Workplace Model™ (SWM) operationalizes SRT within the day-to-day functions of an organization. It addresses how trust, communication, decision-making, and feedback are institutionalized within organizations.

Key Functions of SWM:

- Conflict Recovery Protocols
- Transparent Communication Practices
- Feedback Systems (Top-down, Bottom-up, Peer-to-peer)
- Relational Onboarding
- Team-Based Recognition Rhythms
- Cross-functional Collaboration Routines

🛠 Why it matters:

Too many organizations rely on charismatic leaders instead of cultural structure. SWM ensures that trust, communication, and safety remain intact even if leadership changes.

4.5.3. Symbiotic Leadership Framework™ (SLF)

The External Structure – Leadership in Action

The Symbiotic Leadership Framework™ (SLF) translates SRT and SWM into 12 concrete leadership principles that guide behavior, strategy, and cultural development at all levels. It's where vision becomes practice.

12 Principles of Symbiotic Leadership™:

1. Mutual Empowerment
2. Shared Vision & Purpose
3. Accountability with Grace
4. Emotional Safety
5. Reciprocal Feedback Loops
6. Transparent Communication
7. Distributed Leadership
8. Rhythmic Recognition
9. Constructive Conflict
10. Adaptable Alignment
11. Legacy Mindset
12. Sacred Stewardship

Each principle is designed to scale across:

- C-Suite strategy
- Mid-Level execution
- Frontline engagement

Why it matters:
The SLF provides leaders at every level with a **repeatable** and **reliable structure** for building relational equity, fostering innovation, and developing resilient, values-based leadership cultures.

4.5.4 The Fractal Alignment™

These three layers are not steps; they are simultaneous realities, just as the structure of a galaxy mirrors the structure of a seashell, SRT, SWM, and SLF mirror and sustain one another in every layer of an organization.

SRT   Forms the beliefs & behaviors that create trust

SWM Embeds those beliefs into repeatable systems

SLF   Applies those systems through principled action

This layered model accomplishes what few others do: it integrates leadership into the relational DNA of the workplace.

CHAPTER 5
WHAT WE'VE BUILT
A Unified Model for Relational, Scalable, and Symbiotic Leadership

Chapter 5: What We've Built

A Unified Model for Relational, Scalable, and Symbiotic Leadership™

In this book, we have created something that goes beyond a mere leadership methodology; we have meticulously constructed a complex and adaptable ecosystem along with a pioneering leadership paradigm. This innovative framework is deeply rooted in one of humanity's most ancient and enduring truths: we are innately designed to thrive in harmony with one another. Our exploration reveals how collaborative strength and shared purpose can unlock unparalleled potential, fostering a rich tapestry of connection and growth that benefits both individuals and communities.

The journey began with the deep understanding that symbiosis goes beyond just biological existence; it embodies a universal principle that influences all life forms. From the immense galaxies swirling in the universe to solar systems gracefully moving in their elliptical paths, and from the close-knit connections of families to the engaging interactions within teams and organizations, all that is lively and growing thrives on mutual investment, ongoing feedback loops, and a collective sense of purpose.

When leadership fully embraces this inspired design, it transcends mere practice to become a powerful catalyst for meaningful change. This transformation elevates it from a functional role to a profound force that can instigate significant shifts in the lives of individuals and entire communities. The impact of such leadership resonates deeply, inspiring growth, fostering collaboration, and igniting a sense of purpose that can reshape lives and drive collective advancement.

5.1 We Introduced the Three Spheres of Symbiotic Leadership™:

1. **Symbiotic Relationship Theory™ (SRT):**
   The inner core is the belief system that human flourishing is built on emotional safety, reciprocal accountability, and mutual growth. This theory provides the relational DNA every organization needs.

2. **Symbiotic Workplace Model™ (SWM):**
   The middle sphere is the operational system that carries the culture. SWM translates relational trust into structure: feedback loops, onboarding rhythms, collaboration rituals, and conflict recovery processes.

3. **Symbiotic Leadership Framework™ (SLF):**
   The outer layer is the actionable framework, defined by **12 Symbiotic Leadership Principles™**, guiding behavior at every level of the organization. These principles align vision with action, character with culture, and values with execution.

Each layer reflects and reinforces the other, just as a fractal pattern maintains form from the macro to the micro. What starts in theory becomes practice. What begins in a relationship becomes a system. What takes root in the heart of a leader radiates outward to transform an entire organization.

We Explored the 12 Principles That Anchor the Model:

From Mutual Empowerment and Shared Vision to Sacred Stewardship and a Legacy Mindset, these principles transcend leadership ideals; they represent relational disciplines.

They are scalable, measurable, and repeatable, aimed at replacing isolated leadership with relational symmetry and changing transactional management into transformational belonging.

The principles were not just theorized; they were applied across levels:

- **C-Suite** strategy and direction
- **Mid-level** execution and alignment
- **Frontline** engagement and culture-building

This structure is not fragile. It is **built on a scale**, like the universe itself.

We Created the Tools to Apply It:

In this book, readers were not only inspired by a vision—they were equipped with:

- A **Principles Matrix** outlining application across leadership tiers
- A **Fractal Leadership Diagram** visualizing the model in 3D
- A framework that integrates **emotion, ethics, systems, and scalability**
- A pathway to implementation without sacrificing authenticity or agility

This isn't just a framework; it is a leadership ecosystem that breathes, adapts, and renews itself as long as its relational core remains intact.

5.2 Real-World Implications of Adopting This Model

What Changes When We Lead Relationally

Embracing the Symbiotic Leadership™ model goes beyond a simple transformation in internal company culture; it signifies a comprehensive strategic realignment that profoundly impacts organizational performance and success. In an increasingly complex landscape marked by burnout and fragmentation, organizations that prioritize relational structures develop a distinctive competitive advantage, nurturing a vibrant cultural identity and strengthening human connection.

While many companies focus on efficiency, optimization, or groundbreaking innovation, Symbiotic Leadership™ creates rich environments where these goals emerge naturally. Organizations can unlock their full potential by fostering a foundation of trust, encouraging empowerment, and promoting shared ownership, allowing creativity and collaboration to thrive sustainably.

From Transactional to Transformational Cultures

In traditional organizations, leadership frequently hinges on the allure of charisma, the rigidity of top-down control, or the reliance on operational checklists. While these approaches may yield immediate results, they often fall short in fostering genuine, sustained engagement among team members. Such systems tend to prioritize short-term objectives over nurturing a culture of collaboration and innovation, ultimately leading to a lack of lasting impact and disengagement in the long run.

Symbiotic Leadership™ replaces control with connection, replacing burnout with belonging.

Traditional Culture	Symbiotic Culture
Command-and-control management	Shared ownership and mutual responsibility
Information hoarding	Transparent communication and knowledge flow
Isolated leaders	Distributed influence and feedback loops
Reactive performance management	Proactive emotional safety and growth rhythms
Individual recognition culture	Rhythmic, team-based celebration

The Cost of Maintaining Old Systems

Organizations that fail to adopt relationally intelligent leadership face significant hidden costs:

- **Turnover:** Employees leave managers, not jobs, especially when emotional safety and feedback are missing.
- **Siloed innovation:** When ideas are trapped in vertical structures, innovation slows.
- **Low trust:** Without transparency and mutual accountability, teams become compliance-focused, not mission-focused.

- **Burnout & disengagement:** Emotional labor with no relational replenishment leads to disengaged, transactional work.

Symbiotic Leadership™ directly addresses each of these issues by building systems where human value and organizational value are aligned.

The Benefits of Symbiotic Leadership™ in Practice

When implemented consistently, Symbiotic Leadership™ creates tangible, measurable outcomes:

Area	Outcome
Engagement	Employees feel seen, heard, and invested
Innovation	Psychological safety boosts creative risk-taking
Retention	High-trust cultures retain talent longer
Collaboration	Teams function with clarity and care
Execution	A shared vision improves alignment and outcomes
Leadership Pipeline	Empowerment grows new leaders from within

Whether you lead a five-person startup or a global enterprise, these outcomes scale because the model is founded on a universal principle: healthy systems thrive when relationships are prioritized.

Organizational Systems That Transform

Adopting this model means leaders must not only think differently but also build differently. The implications include:

- **Feedback isn't optional**; it's rhythmic and multidirectional.
- **Recognition isn't performance-only**; it includes emotional labor, support, and alignment.
- **Accountability isn't punishment**; it's a process of grace and recalibration.
- **Meetings aren't status checks**; they're relational checkpoints and purpose aligners.
- **Strategy isn't top-down**; it's ecosystem-informed and bottom-up reinforced.

These practices demand bravery, steadfastness, and a leadership team dedicated to the gradual and sustainable process of cultivating culture.

5.2 Summary

Adopting Symbiotic Leadership™ means embracing a new pattern for performance, one where people are not simply managed but multiplied, not just retained but reinvigorated.

The real-world implications include:

- Healthier systems
- Healthier people
- Healthier long-term results

But the most profound shift is this:
Leadership becomes less about outcomes and more about ecosystems.
And in healthy ecosystems, growth is not forced; it's inevitable.

5.3 A Call for Courage and Cultural Renewal

Why the Future Belongs to the Brave

Transforming our approach to leadership is not just a matter of fine-tuning existing techniques; it requires a deep commitment to courage. It necessitates the bravery to challenge long-standing traditions and the strength to trust individuals, promote transparency, and engage in relational leadership within environments that have historically prioritized hierarchy and self-preservation.

Symbiotic Leadership™ requires a major internal transformation among leaders before they can effectively drive external change. This approach encourages leaders to set aside their egos in favor of genuine empathy, to replace traditional authority with a culture of shared accountability, and to move away from reactive command-and-control structures towards a dynamic framework based on trust and reciprocity.

This evolution in leadership style does not indicate weakness; rather, it embodies the most courageous form of leadership. It emphasizes leading through connection and collaboration instead of control, advocating for a model where relationships thrive, and prioritizing collective success over individual power. By embracing these principles, leaders not only enhance their effectiveness but also foster an environment where innovation and mutual support can flourish.

The Crisis of Culture

The modern workplace is facing a quiet crisis. It's not just about disengagement or turnover, it's about disconnection.

- Leaders feel isolated at the top.
- Managers are caught in the middle, overwhelmed and under-supported.
- Employees often feel unseen, unheard, and underutilized.

Culture, when left uncurated, inevitably drifts into a state of mere survival. In this survival-mode existence, cultures become transactional, steeped in cynicism, and inherently fragile. They come to view individuals not as dynamic, living systems with unique needs and aspirations, but rather as interchangeable labor units, stripped of their humanity and depth. Over time, this approach leads to a gradual unraveling, as the weight of misalignment, exhaustion, and pervasive fear takes its toll, ultimately causing the cultural fabric to collapse.

This is the moment to choose a new model.

Culture Is Built One Brave Leader at a Time

No consultant, framework, or slide deck can transform an organization's culture if its leaders won't model the change themselves.

That's why Symbiotic Leadership™ starts with you, not your systems.
It starts in conversations, not policies.
It shows up in how you handle:

- A team member's mistake
- A missed target
- A tense disagreement
- A moment where grace and truth must both be present

Each of these moments is an invitation:
To lead with courage.
To build culture on connection.
To choose growth through reciprocity, not dominance.

The Leader's Mandate

You don't need a new title to lead cultural renewal.
You need a new mindset and the willingness to act with relational courage.

That means:

- Leading listening sessions even when you're afraid of feedback
- Naming dysfunction without shaming people
- Restoring accountability where fear has silenced honesty
- Making belonging and emotional safety as essential as KPIs and OKRs

5.3 Summary

The future is not defined by organizations that excel in technical efficiency. It is shaped by leaders who demonstrate remarkable relational courage. Those who actively choose to embody and reflect a universal fractal of trust, alignment, and collective growth across all levels of their teams. These visionary leaders cultivate an environment where meaningful connections thrive, encouraging collaboration and a shared purpose that elevates not just their organizations but also the individuals within them.

This isn't a trend. It's a calling. This isn't just leadership; this is Symbiotic Leadership™.

5.4 Reflection Questions for Leaders and Organizations

Cultivating Clarity, Courage, and Change

True leadership transformation doesn't start with the introduction of new policies or procedures; it begins with the art of asking insightful questions. These questions should be honest, vulnerable, and even disruptive, encouraging us to delve deeply into our practices and beliefs. They invite us to reflect not only on our actions but also on the very essence of who we are as a leadership culture. By fostering this level of introspection, we can cultivate an environment where growth and meaningful change can truly flourish.

Use the following prompts as a guide for personal reflection, executive retreats, or team-based discussion forums.

The goal is not perfection. The goal is alignment, authenticity, and relational courage.

5.4.1 Self-Reflection Questions for Individual Leaders

1. Where in my leadership have I prioritized control over connection?
2. Do my people feel safe enough to bring me honest feedback? If not, why?
3. What leadership patterns have I inherited that no longer reflect who I want to be?
4. Which of the 12 Symbiotic Leadership™ Principles do I naturally embody—and which do I resist?
5. When was the last time I apologized as a leader? What did that moment produce?
6. Is my influence sustained by relationship or by role and authority?
7. What would change if I viewed leadership as stewardship rather than ownership?
8. What emotional culture do I actively create or passively allow?
9. Where am I avoiding a hard conversation that, if handled well, could build trust?
10. Who has helped me grow, and how am I multiplying that growth in others?

5.4.2 Team/Organizational Culture Questions

1. Is our culture safe enough for truth to be spoken and trust to be repaired?
2. How well do our systems (performance reviews, recognition, onboarding) reflect relational values?
3. Do we celebrate only outcomes, or do we also recognize emotional labor, alignment, and team contributions?
4. Is feedback multidirectional, or do certain voices consistently dominate or disappear?
5. What processes do we have in place for resolving healthy conflict? Are they relational or punitive?
6. Where does our organization rely on personality over principle?
7. Do we treat culture as an afterthought or as a strategic foundation?
8. What part of our leadership identity needs to be reimagined to align with the future?
9. Are we developing leaders who replicate relational health, or just technical competence?
10. If every team in our organization perfectly mirrored our culture, would we be proud of the result?

How to Use These Questions

- **Individually**: Journal through them in solitude, then revisit monthly.
- **In Teams**: Choose 2–3 prompts per quarter for open discussion.
- **In Leadership Development**: Use as part of onboarding or training for future leaders.
- **In Retreats or Workshops**: Facilitate courageous, structured reflection for alignment and healing.

Final Reminder

These questions are not a test. They are a mirror.
Not to shame, but to sharpen.
Not to disrupt for the sake of disruption but to renew what's been dulled by routine.

If you lean into them fully, these questions won't just shift your mindset; they'll reshape your leadership identity from the inside out.

5.5 Tools – Equipping Your Culture for Symbiotic Leadership™

Vision without the right tools can lead to deep frustration and unrealized potential. This is precisely why Symbiotic Leadership™ transcends mere theoretical concepts; it serves as a comprehensive toolkit designed for cultural transformation. Crafted for practical application, it integrates seamlessly into onboarding processes, training programs, assessment frameworks, and long-term strategic initiatives.

The tools outlined in this section are designed to help organizations assess their alignment with core values, strengthen team relationships, and effectively implement the 12 Symbiotic Principles across every leadership tier. By leveraging these resources, organizations can cultivate a thriving environment where vision and execution are aligned.

CHAPTER 6
LEADING THE FUTURE
with Symbiotic Leadership

Chapter 6: Leading the Future with Symbiotic Leadership™

6.1 A Commission of Conviction, Culture, and Calling

Symbiotic Leadership™ transcends traditional frameworks, offering a transformative perspective on the intricate connections among individuals, shared goals, and power dynamics. This viewpoint examines the nuances of relational interactions, integrating restorative approaches and innovative, scalable methods that foster growth and understanding. Originating as a theoretical idea, it has matured into a potent reflection of our fundamental values, a fluid model that informs our actions, and an energetic movement that drives meaningful change within our communities. By adopting this approach, you don't just modify your leadership style; you radically rethink the core motivations behind your leadership, the communities you uplift, and the enduring legacy you aspire to create. Symbiotic Leadership™ invites a deep exploration of the relationships you foster, the significant impacts you aim to achieve, and the brighter future you envision for those you guide—a future rooted in collaboration, empathy, and mutual success.

6.2 The Invitation to Transformation

This leadership model transcends the notion of control. Rather, it embodies the essence of growth and mutuality in the universe. You are granted the unique opportunity to lead in a manner that mirrors the fundamental nature of the universe, intrinsically relational, fostering mutual dependence, and possessing an inherent capacity for growth and scalability.

Embrace this journey of leadership as one where collaboration and interconnectedness thrive, reflecting the beautiful tapestry of existence itself.

Transformation starts when a leader:

- Humble themselves enough to listen
- Owns the influence they carry
- Steward the emotional safety of others
- Rebuild what culture has neglected

This is not just personal change. It's an invitation to become a mirror of Symbiotic Leadership™.

6.3 *Visualization of Symbiotic Leadership Framework™*

Symbiosis: Utilizing Symbiotic Leadership™ to Guide and Improve Relationships

Fractal Alignment™
based on universal fractal
symbiotic design

Fractal Alignment™

Fractal Alignment™ reveals a design mirrored in the universe, from galaxies to ecosystems to human relationships. These repeating structures showcase intentionality in interdependence. This image introduces the theological and structural foundation for all that follows, establishing fractal alignment as the blueprint for symbiotic leadership.

The Symbiotic Leadership Framework™

The Symbiotic Leadership Framework™ is the first 3D leadership model built on the concept of fractal alignment. At the center lies Symbiotic Relationship Theory™, surrounded by the operational core of the Symbiotic Workplace Model™ and encircled by the guiding leadership framework. This structure embodies how philosophy, behavior, and structure align symbiotically.

The 12 Symbiotic Leadership Principles™

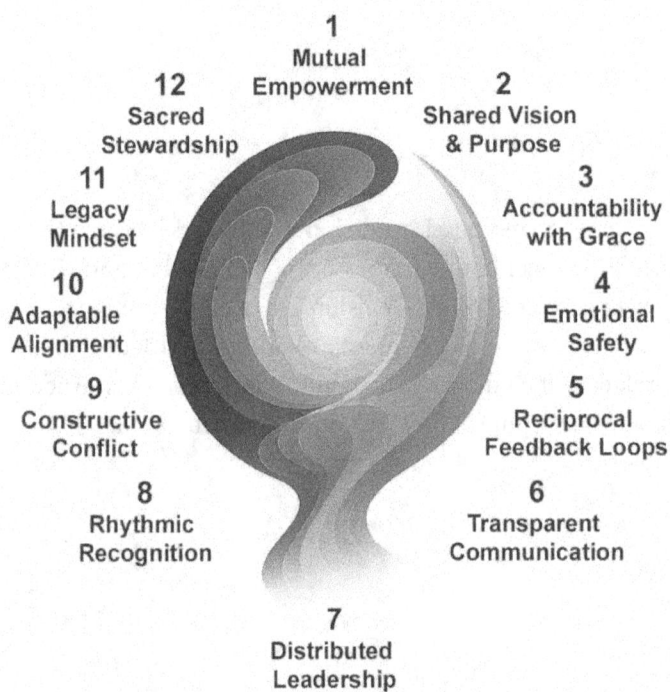

The 12 Symbiotic Leadership Principles™

From the Symbiotic Leadership Framework™ emerge the 12 Symbiotic Leadership Principles™. A set of guiding relational behaviors that scale from self to system. Each principle reflects the values of trust, alignment, and stewardship, offering practical ways to lead with grace and purpose while maintaining relational health at all levels.

The Core Pillars of Symbiotic Relationship Theory™

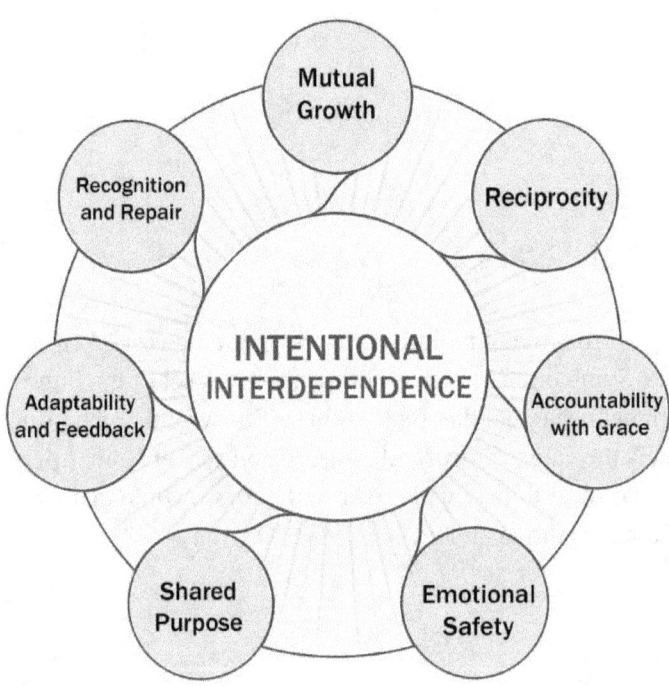

The Core Pillars of Symbiotic Relationship Theory™

The Core Pillars of Symbiotic Relationship Theory™ form the theological and relational backbone of the framework. Mutual Growth, Reciprocity, Accountability with Grace, and Emotional Safety are just a few of the anchors that uphold intentional interdependence. These values are not abstract. They are embedded in daily interactions and leadership practices.

Key Functions of the
SYMBIOTIC WORKPLACE MODEL™

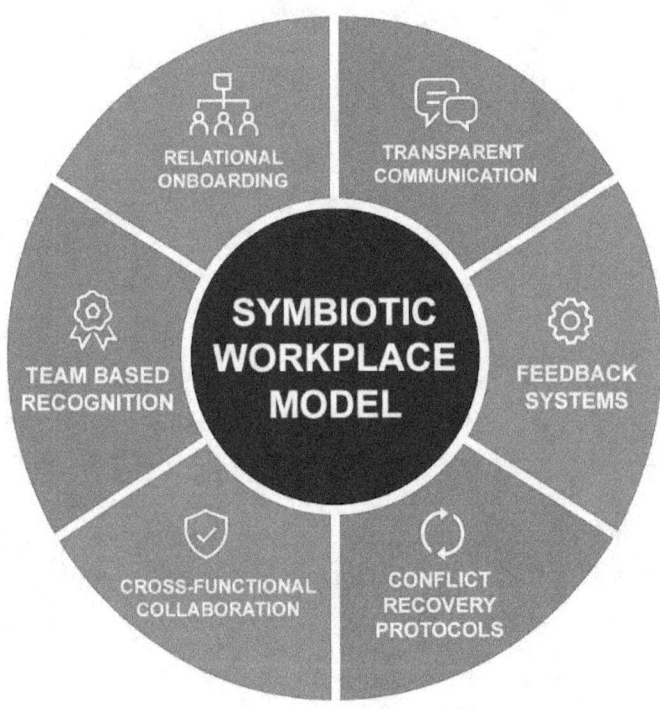

The Symbiotic Workplace Model™

The Symbiotic Workplace Model™ expresses Symbiotic Relationship Theory™ in motion. This wheel visualizes the key relational functions of the model: conflict recovery, feedback systems, recognition rhythms, and relational onboarding. These aren't policies, they are patterns that keep the workplace in relational alignment.

Symbiotic Workplace Model Structure™

The Symbiotic Workplace Model Structure™

The Symbiotic Workplace Model Structure™ is a fractal of trust, collaboration, and accountability that operates at every layer of the organization. Leadership empowers teams, which in turn empower employees, and the system reinforces itself through transparent feedback loops. This diagram shows how symbiosis flows continuously, mirroring the same fractal alignment that shapes the cosmos.

The Symbiotic Mentorship Cycle™

The Symbiotic Mentorship Cycle illustrates the universal sequence of mutual growth through guided reflection, shared knowledge, and consistent feedback. This cycle creates a relational loop of transformation that highlights a fractal of moving from information to transformation, over and over again.

The Symbiotic Human Relationship Cycle™

Relationships are built through recurring acts of connection, vulnerability, trust, and grace. This visual captures the living flow of human symbiosis—the constant exchange that leads to personal and relational transformation. At its core, it reflects universal design: relational, redemptive, and resilient.

The Symbiotic Organizational Leadership Cycle™

Vision

Empowerment

Recognition

Repeat

Reflection

The Symbiotic Organizational Leadership Cycle™

Organizational leadership is not linear. It is cyclical, relational, and adaptive. This diagram illustrates how vision leads to collaboration, collaboration leads to empowerment, and empowerment ultimately yields results. Recognition and reflection close the loop and restart the rhythm. It is a fractal of relational leadership at scale.

Lead with intention.

Stop waiting for permission to model relational health.

Build what reflects the Universe.

Create systems that reward collaboration, communication, and covenantal care.

Embody the pattern.

Be a fractal of the Universe — small, repeating, and constant.

Let your leadership be more than effective.

>Let it be **transformational**. Let it be **sacred**. Let it be **symbiotic**.

Thank you for exploring these new concepts, future Symbiotic Leaders.

Glossary

Symbiotic Relationship Theory™ (SRT)

A relational theory that views connection as an ecosystem. It asserts that healthy relationships—personal or professional—require mutual benefit, interdependence, and intentionality. SRT focuses on the long-term cultivation of shared growth, not transactional interaction.

Symbiotic Workplace Model™ (SWM)

A circular organizational model designed to operationalize SRT within teams and institutions. It replaces rigid hierarchies with relational flow, promoting a culture where feedback, trust, facilitation, and autonomy are encouraged at every level.

Symbiotic Leadership™

A framework for leadership that is rooted in trust, alignment, empathy, accountability, and the development of others. It seeks to influence through connection rather than control, leading relationally rather than transactionally.

Symbiotic Leadership Principles™

A set of twelve guiding values, including Intentional Alignment, Mutual Accountability, Empathetic Communication, and Scalable Growth. These principles act as a compass for relational decision-making and team development.

Fractal Alignment™

A visual and conceptual metaphor for how relational systems (like galaxies, solar systems, ecosystems, and teams) reflect repeating patterns. In Symbiosis, Fractal Alignment™ is the idea that leadership behaviors and relational values can scale harmoniously across all levels of influence.

Relational Symmetry™

The condition in which all parties in a relationship feel seen, heard, valued, and respected. It reinforces equality in contributions and outcomes, allowing trust and collaboration to flourish.

SRT → SWM → SLF

This flow represents the architecture of the Symbiotic model:

- **SRT** is the theory and worldview.
- **SWM** is how the theory is structured within the workplace.
- **SLF** (Symbiotic Leadership Framework™) is how leadership behavior operationalizes both.

For more information on Symbiotic Leadership, Symbiotic Relationship Theory, the Symbiotic Workplace Model, or Fractal Alignment, and for further details and look out for future releases, please visit www.mysybiosis.com.

www.ingramcontent.com/pod-product-compliance
Lightning Source LLC
Chambersburg PA
CBHW050208240426
43671CB00013B/2257